THINKING CRITICALLY ABOUT MEDIA AND POLITICS

THINKING CRITICALLY ABOUT MEDIA AND POLITICS

Donald Lazere

Paradigm Publishers
Boulder • London

All rights reserved. No part of this publication may be transmitted or reproduced in any media or form, including electronic, mechanical, photocopy, recording, or informational storage and retrieval systems, without the express written consent of the publisher.

Copyright © 2013 by Paradigm Publishers

Published in the United States by Paradigm Publishers, 5589 Arapahoe Avenue, Boulder, CO 80303 USA.

Paradigm Publishers is the trade name of Birkenkamp & Company, LLC, Dean Birkenkamp, President and Publisher.

Library of Congress Cataloging-in-Publication Data

Lazere, Donald.
  Thinking critically about media and politics / Donald Lazere.
    pages cm
  Includes bibliographical references and index.
  ISBN 978-1-61205-274-8 (pbk. : alk. paper)
  1. Mass media—Political aspects—United States.   2. Press and politics—United States.   3. Critical thinking—United States.   I. Title.
  P95.82.U6L39 2013
  302.230973—dc23
                                                                    2012046075

Printed and bound in the United States of America on acid-free paper that meets the standards of the American National Standard for Permanence of Paper for Printed Library Materials.

17 16 15 14 13   1 2 3 4 5

Contents

Chapter 1	Introduction: An Appeal to Students	1
Chapter 2	Thinking Critically about Political Rhetoric	23
Chapter 3	Thinking Critically about Mass Media	59
Chapter 4	Special Interests and Propaganda	85
Chapter 5	Advertising and Hype	103
Chapter 6	Analyzing Economic Arguments and Statistical Trickery	115
Appendix	Glossary of Logical and Rhetorical Fallacies	141
	Directory of Political Media★	
Bibliography		151
Index		155

★On the web at www.paradigmpublishers.com/Books/BookDetail.aspx?productID=321369

1

Introduction

An Appeal to Students

Our culture places huge value on physical fitness. The media are filled every day with ads for building muscles or working off fat, and with dramatic images of self-defense. There are not many ads for, or dramatizations of, building our mental muscles, reducing the fat in our brain, or defending ourselves in argumentation. Shouldn't we be able to fight back against those trying to take verbal and intellectual advantage of us? This book is a survival guide for self-defense against manipulation by political, commercial, and other varieties of propaganda, as communicated through mass media.

The book is a spin-off of *Reading and Writing for Civic Literacy: The Critical Citizen's Guide to Argumentative Rhetoric,* a textbook primarily for the second term of first-year English classes or a more advanced course in argumentative writing. This version places less emphasis on the writing dimension and formal exposition of rhetorical terminology, in the hope that it will be useful in a wider range of college courses, including the social sciences, journalism, communications, and media criticism—in which it could be read either as a central text or as a supplement to more discipline-specific books. Exercises at the end of sections stimulate thought, discussion, research, and writing assignments. Because much of the analysis of political arguments throughout the book emphasizes common fallacies in reasoning, the Appendix contains a glossary of logical fallacies, and the terms in that list are boldfaced throughout the text.

In recent years, best-seller lists have been filled with liberal and conservative polemics like Ann Coulter's *Slander: Liberal Lies about the American Right* and Al Franken's *Lies and the Lying Liars Who Tell Them: A Fair and Balanced Look at the Right.* This phenomenon recalls George Orwell's judgment in "Politics and the English Language": "In our age, there is no such thing as 'keeping out of politics.' All issues are political issues, and politics itself is a mass of lies, evasions, folly, hatred and schizophrenia" (*Orwell's Nineteen Eighty-Four,* 256). Especially with the proliferation in the past few decades of partisan media of news and commentary on TV, radio, and the Internet, many Americans have been able to expose themselves only to sources of information that they already agree with and to shut out any contradictory viewpoints. (Even the most highly educated, scrupulous thinkers are innately captive to egocentric and ethnocentric biases on public controversies, needing to struggle constantly against those biases.) Those on the right and left shrilly accuse the other side of diabolically deceptive, monopolistic control of American politics, media, culture, and education, while portraying their own side as powerless, persecuted, and wholly virtuous. All sides claim to have irrefutable evidence proving they are telling the truth and their opponents are lying. So what are we to make of this dizzying, vicious circle of accusation? How can we possibly distinguish truth-tellers from liars?

This book aims to approach these questions through the application of principles of critical thinking and argumentative rhetoric—defined as the study of elements and patterns of persuasion, both scrupulous and unscrupulous ones (though popular usage tends to equate rhetoric solely with the latter). This approach to critical thinking and rhetoric also draws heavily from the study of semantics––emphasizing the role in argumentation of definition or denotation of terms, verbal slanting, and emotional appeal through connotative language, what I term **cleans and dirties**. For example, compare the different connotative "spins" in two responses to a 2007 U.S. Treasury Department report on trends in income mobility in America during the previous decade. An editorial in the conservative *Wall Street Journal* said, "Of those in the second lowest income quintile, nearly 50% moved into the middle quintile or higher.... This is a stunning show of upward mobility, meaning that more than half of all lower-income Americans in 1996 had moved up the income scale in only 10 years." But liberal columnist Eugene Robinson in the *Washington Post,* looking at the same figures, wrote, "An incredible 42 percent of children born into that lowest quintile are still stuck at the bottom, having been unable to climb a single rung of the income ladder."

Semantic misunderstandings constantly result from liberals' and conservatives' different subjective viewpoints on, definitions of, and connotative spins on, the very words *liberal* and *conservative,* as well as related words like *capitalism, socialism,* and *democracy.* President Obama was widely identified by conservatives in polls as a "socialist," "communist," or "Marxist," although such polls rarely asked the respondents how they defined those terms or what evidence justified them. At the same time, many liberals were denouncing Obama for selling out to Wall Street capitalists and for continuing the same conservative policies as President Bush on the wars in Afghanistan and Iraq, national security, and domestic surveillance. Chapter 2 approaches such semantic misunderstandings by presenting a glossary of political terms like these in all their complexities, ambiguities, and points of disagreement; the aim is to arrive at definitions that are agreed on by both liberals and conservatives, or leftists and rightists, so that they can at least agree about what they disagree about. Semantic study also emphasizes the open-ended nature of controversies between, say, conservatives and liberals. The journal of the Institute for General Semantics is titled *et cetera,* reflecting the principle that there is rarely any "last word" in such controversies but only a continuous sequence of rebuttals and counter-rebuttals. So at several points in the book students are asked explicitly or implicitly to try to find arguments that refute the arguments presented here.

POLITICS IS INTERESTED IN *YOU*

Thinking critically about politics and media has not been a central part of many modern Americans' education or cultural formation. In fact, everything in our culture seems calculated to focus our thinking on anything *but* politics. At the very mention of the word "politics," many students start groaning, "I'm just not interested in politics." As a plea to persuade you not to turn off, let me argue that "politics" doesn't just refer to dry matters of the branches of government, the structure of parties and electoral processes, and such. Many Americans believe their life and work are wholly personal matters and under their own control, and thus they can ignore what happens in the public sphere; to the extent they are aware of larger national or international forces, they believe that those forces are beyond their understanding or control, hence not worth thinking about. You may not think you are interested in politics; however, politics is interested in *you*.

Americans were especially shocked by the events of September 11, 2001, because many had little or no knowledge of the Al Qaeda terrorist organization, the location of Afghanistan and Iraq where we were soon plunged into war, or the long-term political conflicts in the Middle East and Central Asia that were necessary background for full understanding of these events. Among the reactions to the attacks was a widespread recognition that this was a wake-up call for Americans to make much more effort to educate themselves about historical and current events throughout the world, especially those in which America's government, military, and corporations are directly involved and in which the consequences of that involvement can change any of our personal lives. When the United States invaded Iraq in 2003, tens of thousands of young men and women in the armed services, many of whom had entered the military mainly for its vocational or educational opportunities, found themselves fighting in a distant part of the world for a cause they knew little about, other than what they had been indoctrinated in by their commanding officers, and in a foreign culture about whose language, religion, and customs they knew even less about. All these issues surrounding 9/11 and Iraq are "politics."

Shortly after teaching an American literature survey course at the University of Tennessee in spring 2004, in which we had briefly discussed the Iraq war in relation to Henry David Thoreau's "Essay on Civil Disobedience," I received the following e-mail from a student in the class:

> I just wanted to tell you that I have gotten much more into politics since I started your class and feel that it has become more important to me now that I am getting older. The events in Iraq over the last few months have disturbed me very much in relation to the prisoner abuse and the beheadings. In addition, one of my closest friends from high school was killed in Iraq over the weekend and his death has very much disturbed me since I was so close to him. He was a U.S. Marine stationed and killed in Fallujah, and now I have another good friend who is being sent back to Iraq in the next few weeks. Now, I feel like all of this mess in Iraq was pointless and I am frustrated that my friend laid down his life for a fiasco. I finally feel like the whole situation in

Iraq has become very real to me after his death. It is very scary when people mention the possibility of a draft after a tragedy like this. I only wish we could have talked more about this in your class during the past semester.

Politics further includes controversies about *money,* a subject that interests everyone. We live today in a political economy in which personal concerns like the cost of living, availability of jobs, access to and cost of health care, tax policy, placement of and return on our investments (especially retirement pensions), are determined by national and international forces that we cannot afford to ignore. The concentration of corporate ownership in recent decades, the growing gap in the distribution of income, power, and taxation between the rich and the middle class and poor, and between big business and small, individual businesses—all of these directly influence everyone's daily life. Your ability to find a job in the location of your choice, and at the salary of your choice, may be determined by corporate mergers, downsizing, automation, movement of industries globally into cheap labor markets, and bankruptcies like those of Enron and Worldcom in the early 2000s and a whole host of financial institutions by 2010. Your family business or farm may be subject to a corporate takeover, or at least be affected by fluctuations in international stock and monetary markets, competition from companies that have moved to Third World countries with lower operating costs, or other forces in the global economy. As a character in the 1976 film *Network* puts it, "The totality of life on this planet" is now determined by "one vast and immane, interwoven, interacting, multi-variate, multinational dominion of dollars.... We are no longer an industrialized society; we aren't even a post-industrial or technological society. We are now a corporate society, a corporate world, a corporate universe" (130–135).

You are certainly concerned about the increasingly high cost of college tuition, textbooks, and housing; how much financial aid is available to you and at what cost; what part-time jobs are available to you as a student, how much they pay, and—above all—what your occupational and financial prospects are after you graduate. But how are public policies on all these matters determined, and by whom? Not by impersonal, uncontrollable forces like the weather. They are mostly controlled by human agents, by struggles for dominance between opposing political parties and ideologies (an ideology is a system of political concepts, such as liberalism and conservatism, or of economic concepts like capitalism and socialism); between interests representing corporate management versus those of employees;

between the public sector (government employees, schools and colleges, and other nonprofit organizations) and the private, for-profit sector (corporations and small businesses, professions like law and medicine); between supporters of a planned economy and of the free market, and so on. Whether you ever become conscious of it or not, you have the choice to become aware of the workings of all these forces and to attempt actively to influence them, or to go through a life controlled by them without your ever understanding or exerting any influence on them.

Beyond controversies over political economy, other issues like environmentalism, feminism and racism, affirmative action, abortion, gun control, and capital punishment are sometimes perceived as political, but it is often far from clear in public disputes over them that they all involve a dimension of partisan politics, along liberal versus conservative or left versus right ideological lines, though not always Democratic versus Republican party lines—as will be explained in Chapter 2. Indeed, a predictable pattern of political rhetoric is for those arguing about such issues to conceal the partisan nature of their arguments under a guise of nonpartisanship. Of course, not all public arguments fall into left versus right oppositions—but a lot *do,* and the failure of many citizens to perceive the nature of these oppositions can leave them without adequate understanding of the issues.

WHO MAKES THE RULES?

The Free Speech Movement at the University of California, Berkeley, in 1964, was set off in part by many students' frustration over the feeling that college education had become a process just to turn them into cogs in the machinery of business, professions, or government. The movement's most eloquent leader, twenty-two-year-old Mario Savio, asserted about the university,

> The best among the people who enter must for four years wander aimlessly much of the time questioning why they are on campus at all, doubting whether there is any point in what they are doing, and looking toward a very bleak existence afterward in a game in which all of the rules have been made up—rules which we can not really amend.... The "futures" and "careers" for which American students now prepare are for the most part intellectual and moral wastelands. This chrome-plated consumers' paradise would have us grow up to be well-behaved children.

Do you too perhaps have the feeling that you are being educated to play a game, vocationally and politically, in which someone else has made all the rules? This book, then, attempts to present a beginning toward the kind of knowledge and critical skills you need, first to learn the language of those who make the rules, and ultimately to become an active participant in making them.

This kind of knowledge and critical skills begins with the value of opening your mind and broadening your perspective on the beliefs with which you were brought up. One way of doing that is to try to look at your beliefs in a new way: in regard to any belief that you are convinced is based on facts or the truth, ask yourself how you came to believe it is true. In other words, what is your viewpoint on it, and how did you acquire that viewpoint? From what sources of information did you get the belief—your family, teachers, peers, church, political leaders, news, entertainment, and advertising media? Others? Where did *those* sources get their beliefs? What might be the limitations or biases in your knowledge, and in that of your sources? Those sources' views are often colored by conscious or unconscious ethnocentrism, self-interest, and ideological biases, to say nothing of outright hype, **propaganda**, and deception on occasion. So we need to develop a critical perspective on *them* to evaluate their reliability. In contrast, then, to the common textbook approach that assumes faulty arguments result only from unintentional lapses in reasoning, this book confronts the hard truth that real-life arguments frequently contain deliberate deception, **special pleading**, partisanship, and out-and-out lying, as well as ideological biases that may be conscious or unconscious. The best safeguard against being taken in by the one-sided views of any particular medium of information, or any ideological line-up of media—liberal, conservative, libertarian, or socialist—is to recognize the need to broaden our acquaintanceship to a broader, more varied scope of media sources, along the lines suggested in Chapters 2 and 3.

Some students and teachers will react against this orientation by complaining that it is too "negative," with all the emphasis on detecting and defending against deceptive, fallacious arguments. If you react this way, I urge you to ask yourself two questions as you are reading: Is this "negative" approach *realistic* in relation to the state of American public discourse? And does it succeed in enabling you to be a more critical and active participant in that discourse? An article titled "You're On Your Own," by Daniel Kadlec, which appeared in *Time* (January 28, 2002) after the collapse of Enron Corporation and its accountancy firm Arthur Andersen, presented an unusually frank acknowledgment—especially in a magazine that has long been a booster of American free enterprise:

> We are now responsible for so many decisions requiring so much homework that many of us feel helpless and paralyzed. The risks of inaction or unwise action are rising, even as many of the professionals on whom we would like to rely for guidance are proving untrustworthy and even corrupt.... We now know we can't trust stock analysts and financial planners, who often get paid more for selling us shaky stocks and mutual funds than for selling us solid ones.... The Enron scandal has shown us or perhaps reminded us that when money is involved, we are truly on our own. (24–25)

Finally, try to keep in mind that the purpose of training yourself to spot fallacious arguments is not to cynically dismiss each side in every dispute as equally fallacious, but to be able to distinguish invalid arguments from valid ones, liars from truth-tellers—so as to inspire you to give your wholehearted support to the truth-tellers.

Another response to the charge of negative thinking is that the prevailing emphasis in American society and education on "positive thinking" and "feeling good about yourself" can sometimes serve the function of ostrich-like **sentimentality** and denial of the gravity of our national problems. This point was addressed in an op-ed (an opinion column on the page opposite the editors' own editorials) by Michael Kinsley in the *Los Angeles Times* (June 22, 2004), following the death of President Reagan, titled "The Trouble with Optimism." Kinsley wrote,

> Thanks to Reagan, optimism is now considered an essential ingredient of any presidential candidate's public self-presentation.... Could there be an emptier claim made on behalf of someone hoping to lead the United States of America than to say that he is "optimistic"? Optimism may or may not be part of the American character, but it is pretty insufficient as either a campaign promise or a governing principle.... If forced to choose between a leader whose vision is clouded by optimism and one clouded by pessimism, there is a good case that pessimism is the more prudent choice. Another name for pessimism is a tragic sensibility. It is a vivid awareness that things can go wrong, and often have done so. An optimist thinks he can pop over to Iraq, knock Saddam Hussein off his perch, establish democracy

throughout the Middle East and be home for dinner. A pessimist knows better.

While in most other democracies students are immersed in public controversies and instruction in debating them from an early age, much American culture and education tend to shelter high school and even college students from such controversies, thereby trying to keep them in the mentality of adolescence rather than leading them toward thinking and acting like adults. Remember Mario Savio's words, "This chrome-plated consumers' paradise would have us grow up to be well-behaved children." Even adults are considered to be like children by many public "leaders." In a controversial article following 9/11, essayist Susan Sontag described the Bush administration's statements after the attacks as "a campaign to infantilize the public." In William Safire's book *Before the Fall,* about his experiences as a speechwriter in the Nixon White House, President Nixon is quoted as saying, "The average American is just like the child in the family" (649), and, "We sophisticates can listen to a speech for a half hour, but after ten minutes, the average guy wants a beer" (315). When Howard Jarvis, sponsor of Proposition 13, the influential 1978 tax-cutting ballot initiative in California, was asked why he spent all his advertising money on TV and radio rather than newspapers, he replied, "People who decide elections today don't read" (quoted in *Los Angeles Times,* February 10, 1980, l).

Let me provide a few exemplary anecdotes from my own experience. In my younger years when I was working as a copy-writing trainee at one of the world's largest advertising agencies, on Madison Avenue in New York, I was assigned to suggest a campaign for the latest model of a brand-name refrigerator. The account executive explained to me, "There's really no difference between this year's model and last year's, but we have to keep putting out a new model every year to hype up profits, and the average housewife is too stupid to know the difference." I worked as a public relations agent (a euphemism for propagandist) for wealthy individuals and corporations, making them look like saints, especially in "damage control" after they had been caught in misbehavior. I also worked in public relations for Dick Clark's "American Bandstand," and backstage at their telecasts, I overheard the adult managers of teenage singing stars snickering contemptuously at their clients' and their audiences' "moronic pimple music." After several years at such jobs, I became ashamed of being an agent of this kind of manipulation (albeit a well-paid one) and decided to go to graduate school in English and prepare instead to teach students how to defend themselves against manipulation. My long years of teaching and writing this book are based on the conviction that the average housewife, or the average American voter, or the average college student, is not "too stupid to know the difference," provided that they receive the encouragement and resources to think critically.

The subject of infantilization illustrates a rhetorical term, *self-fulfilling prophecy,* which refers to a situation in which because people are induced to believe something is true, it becomes true; this is a variant on another term, *vicious circle,* in which an effect of some cause itself reinforces that cause, creating a loop that is difficult to break. In this case, if you treat people like children, many will act like children. After all, it's so much easier to be a child than an adult. Who doesn't prefer candy to vegetables, junk food to a nutritious diet, the teacher who gives you an easy "A" rather than making you work hard for it? Everything in my teaching experience, however, has indicated that although many students at the conscious level prefer everything to be made simple and painless for them, deep down they understand that junk-food education does not help them grow and insults their intelligence. So this book attempts to break the vicious circle of infantilization, by assuming that college-age students want to deal with adult realities and complexities, especially concerning the socioeconomic issues emphasized here—frustrating as they can be. (Older students who have had more hard experience of the world will not need to have this point labored.)

GO TO THE MALL INSTEAD?

Back to the "negative" attitude toward politics and public discourse in this book, it would be hard to outdo the fear and loathing that many American students and adults alike already feel toward politics, which are tied to a widespread attitude: "Politicians are all a bunch of crooks, and politics has gotten so complex and corrupt that it's a waste of time even to think about it. Leave it to the professionals." On the surface, this attitude appears perfectly sensible. When you plunge into political controversies and find that on virtually every issue, not only Democrats and Republicans or liberals and conservatives, but also libertarians and radical leftists (or socialists) present diametrically opposed versions of the truth, each persuasively argued and supported by impressive evidence, a natural reaction is to throw your hands in the air, despair of ever knowing whom you can believe, and go to the beach or mall instead. Moreover, many Americans are kept so busy just scrambling to get the necessary, occupational credentials in school to get a job, and then working at that job while worrying about being able to pay their bills from one month to the next, that they feel they cannot spare the time to take courses about public affairs or inform themselves about what is going on politically, to vote, or to take part in political organizations and activities.

Consider, though, that this reaction is another vicious circle, playing right into the hands of the crooks and the special interests that spend a great deal of money and effort trying to obscure the truth, and that if enough ordinary citizens give up on pursuing the truth and participating in the political process, it will guarantee that the deceitful, corrupt "professionals," with no one keeping tabs on them, become ever more corrupt and win by default of opposition. As the freed slave and abolitionist leader Frederick Douglass put it on the brink of the Civil War in 1857, "Find out just what people will submit to, and you have found out the exact amount of injustice and wrong which will be imposed upon them.... The limits of tyrants are prescribed by the endurance of those whom they oppress" (quoted in Wolfgang Mieder, *"No Struggle, No Progress": Frederick Douglass and His Proverbial Rhetoric,* 31).

The most famous commentary on the principles being developed here is George Orwell's 1946 essay "Politics and the English Language," in which Orwell observed,

> Now, it is clear that the decline of a language must ultimately have political and economic causes; it is not due simply to the bad influence of this or that individual writer. But an effect can become a cause, reinforcing the original cause and producing the same effect in an intensified form, and so on indefinitely. A man may take to drink because he feels himself to be a failure, and then fail all the more completely because he drinks. It is rather the same thing that is happening to the English language. It becomes ugly and inaccurate because our thoughts are foolish, but the slovenliness of our language makes it easier for us to have foolish thoughts. The point is that the process is reversible. Modern English, especially written English, is full of bad habits which spread by imitation and which can be avoided if one is willing to take the necessary trouble. If one gets rid of these habits one can think more clearly, and to think clearly is a necessary first step toward political regeneration. (249)

Orwell is discussing another vicious circle here, using the analogy of the drunkard: the clarity of our language is eroded by political and economic causes that prevail partly because they numb clear thinking about them, and unclear thinking leads to unclear language; but our unclear language itself then becomes a cause for unclear thinking—and for further political decay. Similar vicious circles have been described here: if you treat people like children, they are likely to behave like children; the more that Americans believe politics is hopelessly corrupt and obscure, the more corrupt and obscure it *will* be; and as students are forced by financial and social pressures to specialize in occupational majors at the expense of general education, they deprive themselves of precisely the kind of education they need to understand the causes of those pressures and to launch an organized movement against them. However, Orwell continues, the circle of corrupt politics-thought-language might be broken by our starting to clarify our language. Orwell insists that he is not talking about proper grammar or usage, which are incidental, but about forming words and ideas that accurately correspond to external reality, or "language as an instrument for expressing and not for concealing or preventing thought" (259).

Similarly, perhaps a starting point for American students and citizens to break the vicious circles they are caught in is to develop the critical vocabulary and rhetorical concepts enabling them to understand ideas like *vicious circle*. The thesis of this book, then, is that a framework of rhetorical terms and concepts can provide us with a beginning point for becoming more critical and active citizens, the weapons we need to defend ourselves against infantilization.

Without buying into conspiracy theories, it seems reasonable to conjecture that the tendencies in American politics, media, and education toward keeping people in childlike ignorance, deemphasizing the importance of civic education, and presenting political issues in a superficial, incoherent manner are perpetuated because they serve, directly or indirectly, the interests of those who benefit from maintaining the present hierarchies of power. What is certain is that the pervasiveness and elaborate engineering of both political and commercial propaganda in our time far exceed any past period of history, and that the level of American public rhetoric—mainly under the influence of televised and talk-radio political news (especially on twenty-four-hour-a-day cable networks), debates, and advertising—has been declining steadily toward ever shorter and more irrational "sound bites." The professional consultants who developed the rapid-fire "top-forty-stories" format for local newscasts justified it by claiming, "People who watch television the most are unread, uneducated, untraveled and unable to concentrate on single subjects more than a minute or two" (*San Francisco Examiner and Chronicle,* March 16, 1975, 14).

Political party organizations and government administrations employ television performance consultants and "spin doctors," often from advertising or public relations agencies accustomed to using market research to sell products, who calculate their messages not for their truth value, but for whether they will be "bought" by the largest, least informed segment of the public. So social policies and even wars are now sold like laundry detergent, and prime qualifications for public office are telegenic good looks and acting ability (including the ability to lie convincingly), rather than wisdom and honesty. This situation, in both politics and "entertainment" forms like talk radio, is inevitably a breeding ground for the **demagogue**, a public figure who manipulates the ignorance and prejudices of the masses for his or her own power or profit. (The very fact that so few American students or citizens know the meaning of the word *demagogue* increases their vulnerability to **demagogy**.)

These destructive influences on public discourse are very likely among both the leading causes and effects of the facts confirmed by many recent reports on literacy in the United States, along with books and articles by both conservative and liberal social commentators, indicating an alarmingly low level of interest and knowledge in young Americans of precisely those areas of education—including basic knowledge of history, economics, political science, and sociology—that are most necessary for them to exert democratic control over the forces influencing their lives. Deficiencies in a base of factual knowledge about social science and in critical thinking proficiency in evaluating that knowledge cut across nearly all social segments of American high school and college students. Since the voting age was lowered from twenty-one to eighteen in 1973 (a concession, it should be noted, to the student and anti–Vietnam War protests of the 1960s), the lowest rate of voting has been precisely in the eighteen-to-twenty-one-year-old bracket, and the United States now has the lowest rate of voting of any democracy in the world. This trend was encouragingly reversed in the 2008 and 2012 presidential elections, when many more college students and other young people voted and took an active part in the electoral process, largely in support of Barack Obama.

None of the above bad news is meant to imply that your generation of students is "dumb." It would be a foolhardy **overgeneralization** to suggest that a whole generation was born intellectually deficient. The more valid generalization would be that this generation, by and large, is inadequately educated and informed about politics, through little fault of their own. (To place the fault on *them* is an example of the causal fallacy of blaming the victim.) My experience with students tells me that their indifference toward politics is largely the product of the skimpy amount and quality of the political education they have received; students avoid political issues largely because their education has provided little help in understanding them. Also, as noted earlier, that understanding is made all the more difficult because the discourse of American politics, media, and even education, tends to approach political issues in an incoherent, superficial manner, without providing any explanatory overview of opposing ideologies or viewpoints that would help provide a context for full understanding. I believe most students are perfectly capable of understanding and taking an interest in political issues if those issues are explained in a comprehensible, step-by-step manner, and within a coherent framework of ideological concepts, as this book attempts to do.

Of course, it would not be helpful to pitch this book at a level far above the heads of what most college students who have not taken advanced courses in social science are prepared to understand. The level at which issues are analyzed in this book is that at which they are addressed, not in specialized social science scholarship, but in political speeches, news and entertainment media, op-ed columns, general-circulation journals of opinion, and other realms of public discourse to which everyone is exposed every day. The political vocabulary and information covered here are no more specialized than what every citizen in a democracy should be expected to know. Nevertheless, in Chapter 2, elementary definitions and explanations of political concepts are provided for those students who need them, within the more complex context of analyzing the semantic ambiguity, subjectivity, and relativity that color all of our political viewpoints and language.

At the same time, one of the main points stressed in this book is the difference in levels of rhetoric between public and scholarly treatments of political issues, and the need for students to take courses in more specialized disciplines to pursue deeper knowledge of these issues. Students *can* learn here, though, to develop a more complex and comprehensive rhetorical understanding of political events and ideologies than that provided by politicians and mass media—or, for that matter, by most social science courses, which usually emphasize factual exposition, empirical research, or theory at the expense of rhetorical and semantic analysis.

AVOIDING POLITICAL CORRECTNESS

Finally, an approach like mine can invite the danger of being turned into an indoctrination to the instructor's personal political ideology. This concern has been warranted by the tendency of some "politically correct" teachers (usually liberal or leftist, though there are also cases of conservative political correctness) to assume that all students and colleagues agree—or *should* agree—with their particular view. So one of my main efforts has been to avoid turning this book and the kind of course it is intended for into indoctrination into any particular ideological position. My method in this effort involves addressing as an explicit topic for rhetorical study the issues of political subjectivity, partisanship, and bias in sources of information, including teachers and authors of textbooks—including this one. The principle is that any writer or reader addressing controversial issues will almost inevitably have a subjective, partisan viewpoint (that is, a viewpoint siding with a particular party or ideology). There is nothing wrong with having such a partisan viewpoint; indeed, its clear-cut expression can be a rhetorical virtue in enabling readers to understand what that viewpoint stands for, particularly if the expression is relatively unbiased and supported through sound argumentation. Our aims should simply be to learn to identify and understand what the viewpoint of any given source is, so that we can weigh its rhetorical quality against opposing viewpoints. Furthermore, it is virtually impossible even to define political terms and positions without injecting a partisan opinion into the very definitions—a problem explicitly addressed in Chapter 2.

So we all need to learn to recognize our own ideological viewpoint, and possible biases, as readers and writers, and certainly as teachers. I do not believe that teachers or textbook writers should coyly hide their viewpoint, as they often do, but that they should honestly identify it and present it, not as "the truth" or "the facts" but as one viewpoint among others, needing to be scrutinized for its own biases and fairly evaluated against opposing ones. Thus, although total objectivity may never be attainable, dealing honestly with our own subjectivity may be the best way to approximate objectivity. This principle obliges me to come out from the hiding place of authorial anonymity and pretended objectivity that is the convention in textbooks, and to speak as "I" from time to time throughout the book, especially in addressing issues where it is most difficult for anyone to present an objective, impartial analysis. The intention of this method, then, is to guarantee that students will not be indoctrinated into my own or any teacher's or writer's ideology, but rather that the scope of students' own critical thinking, reading, and writing capacities will be broadened so as to empower them to make their own autonomous judgments on opposing ideological positions in general and on specific issues.

All this being said, it would be hypocritical to deny that the dominant viewpoint in the book is liberal-to-leftist, as defined in Chapter 2, or to deny that this viewpoint most often characterizes college courses in the humanities and social sciences. I suggest that this fact does not indicate a "bias" so much as the justifiable mindset of scholars who devote their careers to a pursuit of knowledge and truth independent of (and providing a critical perspective on) the conservative bias of all the forms of information saturating American society transmitted by corporations (or politicians and educators beholden to corporations), through media of news, commentary, and entertainment that are also owned by corporations and that gain their profits through corporate advertising. My suggestion is more fully supported throughout the book, and like everything else here, it is not put forth as "the last word," but as one viewpoint that is contested by other ones, or as a hypothesis that you can test against evidence pro and con. One thesis of the book is that neither journalists, scholars, nor teachers can or should be expected to be completely balanced, neutral, or nonpartisan in evaluating opposed positions, which often are not equally balanced on their rhetorical merits, or the power of those who propagate them. What *should* be expected is an accurate, fair-minded exposition of what the opposing sides believe and argue, in the course of evaluating the relative merits of their arguments, and qualified by the previously discussed acknowledgment that any judgment posed, explicitly or implicitly, as the last word here can and should be regarded only as a prompt to possible counter-arguments.

This distinctive approach to evaluating public arguments, especially political ones, is visible throughout the book and can be previewed in the following four guides, all of which have multiple applications for students. First, you can apply them to the sources you read in your studies for course work or independently. Second, you can apply them to yourself in your response to what you read and to what you then say about it in discussion or in writing papers. Finally, you can apply them to this book's own viewpoints and its author's possible biases; I always welcome feedback from readers with disagreements or suggestions for refinements, updating, and so on. I can be reached at dlazere@igc.org.

GUIDES FOR ANALYZING POLITICAL ARGUMENTS

Rhetoric: A Checklist for Analyzing Your Own and Others' Arguments

1. When you are expressing your views on a subject, ask yourself how extensive your knowledge of it is, what the sources of that knowledge are, and what restrictions there might be in your vantage point. When you are studying a writer on the subject (or when she cites a source on it), try to figure out what her qualifications are on this particular subject. Is the newspaper, magazine, website, book publisher, or research institute he is writing for (or citing) a reputable one? What is its ideological viewpoint?
2. Are you, as reader or writer (or is the author), indulging in rationalization, or **wishful thinking**—believing something merely because it is what you *want* to believe? In other words, are you distinguishing what is personally advantageous or disadvantageous for you from what you would objectively consider just or unjust?
3. Are the actions of the author, or those she is supporting, consistent with the professed position, or is she saying one thing while doing another? (This is one form of **compartmentalization**, the other most common one being internal inconsistencies in the author's arguments.)
4. Are all of the data ("facts") or quotations correct? Are any data used misleadingly or quotes taken out of context?
5. Semantic issues: Does the author make it clear, either by explicit definition or by context, in exactly what sense she is using any controversial or ambiguous words? In other words, is she using vague, unconcretized abstractions, or is she concretizing her abstractions? Any evasive euphemisms (i.e., "clean" words that obscure a "dirty" truth)?
6. Are the generalizations and assertions of opinion—especially those that are disputable or central to the argument—adequately qualified and supported by reasoning, evidence, or examples? In your own writing, if you haven't been able to provide this support, it may be a good idea not to make these assertions.
7. Is there any unjustifiable (i.e., not supported by adequate evidence) emotional appeal through empty "conditioned

response" words (or "cleans" and "dirties"), **name-calling**, developing of a **straw man**, or innuendo?

8. Are the limits of the position defined or are they vulnerable to being pushed to absurd logical consequences (reduction to absurdity)? In other words, does she indicate where to draw the line?

9. Are all of the analogies (saying two situations are similar) and equations (saying two situations are the same) valid?

10. Does she honestly acknowledge the opposition, fairly balancing all the evidence and arguments of one side against those of the other, giving each side's accurate weight and evaluating them in accurate proportion to each other? (See "Ground Rules for Polemicists" below.)

11. Any faulty causal analyses? Does he view any actions as causes that may really be effects or *reactions*? Any post hoc reasoning—that is, when she asserts that something has happened because of something else, might it be true that the second happened irrespective of, or even in spite of, the first? Has she reduced a probable multiplicity of causes to one (reductionism)? When he argues that a course of action has been unsuccessful because it has been carried too far, might the opposite be true—that it has been unsuccessful because it has not been carried far enough?

12. Other logical fallacies, especially **evading the issue**, **non sequiturs** (conclusions that don't follow logically from the arguments preceding them, or two statements that seem to be related but aren't), **either-or** thinking, false dilemmas, or false dichotomies?

13. Theory versus practice: Are the theoretical proposals practicable or the abstract principles consistent with empirical (verifiable) facts and probabilities, and based on adequate firsthand witness to the situation in question?

A Semantic Calculator for Bias in Rhetoric

This guide (inspired by various versions of Hugh Rank's "Intensify-Downplay Schema") can be applied to reading sources and to writing papers about them, in application to both those sources' biases and to your own.

1. What is the author's vantage point, in terms of social class, wealth, occupation, gender, ethnic group, political ideology,

educational level, age, etc.? Is that vantage point apt to color his attitudes on the issue under discussion? Does he have anything personally to gain from the position he is arguing for, any conflicts of interest or other reasons for special pleading?
2. What organized financial, political, ethnic, or other interests are backing the advocated position? What groups or special interests stand to profit financially, politically, or otherwise from it? In the Latin phrase, *cui bono?*
3. Once you have determined the author's vantage point and the special interests being favored, look for signs of ethnocentrism, rationalization or wishful thinking, sentimentality, one-sidedness, selective vision, or a double standard.
4. Look for the following forms of setting the agenda and **stacking the deck**, reflecting the biases in No. 3:
   a. **Playing up**:
      (1) arguments favorable to one's own side
      (2) arguments unfavorable to the other side
      (3) the other side's power, wealth ("They're only in it for the money"), extremism, misdeeds ("A widespread pattern of abuses"), and unity ("A vast conspiracy," "A tightly-coordinated machine")
   b. **Downplaying** (or suppressing altogether):
      (1) arguments unfavorable to one's own side
      (2) arguments favorable to the other side
      (3) one's own side's power, wealth, extremism, misdeeds ("A small number of isolated instances," "A few rotten apples"), and unity ("An uncoordinated collection of diverse, grassroots groups")
   c. Applying "clean" words (ones with positive connotations) to one's own side, without support; applying "dirty" words (ones with negative connotations) to the other, without support
   d. Assuming that the representatives of one's own side are trustworthy, truthful, and have no selfish motives, while assuming the opposite of the other side
   e. Giving credit to one's own side for positive events; blaming the other side for negative events

This calculator indicates the ways in which we all are inclined, intentionally or unintentionally, to react—often with anger and exaggeration—to our opponents' perceived faults and exercises of power, while not seeing our own side's comparable ones. Of course, emphasizing our side's "good" and the other side's "bad" is a perfectly legitimate part of argumentation, so long as it is done honestly, accurately, with sufficient support, and with a sense of proportion. But good-faith efforts at doing so need to be distinguished from the bad-faith ones of propagandists who stack the deck by deliberately, dishonestly using these techniques to present a simplistic opposition between "good guys" and "bad guys," or of sincere but closed-minded ideologues who resort to the techniques in a knee-jerk conditioned reaction to every public event. In any given case, differential semantic descriptions might serve to make an accurate, supportable judgment on the relative merits of opposing camps—or they might not; it's for you to judge.

So if you don't find blatant signs of the above biases, and if you judge that the emotional language is supported by adequate evidence, that's a good indication that the writer is credible one. If there *are* many such signs, that's a good sign that the writer is not a credible source. However, finding signs of the above biases does not in itself prove that the writer's arguments are fallacious. Don't fall into the **ad hominem** ("against the man") fallacy—evading the issue by attacking the character or motives of the writer or speaker without refuting the substance of the argument itself. What the writer says may or may not be factual, regardless of the semantic biases. The point is not to let yourself be swayed by emotive words alone, especially when you are inclined to wishful thinking on one side of the subject yourself. When you find these biases in other writers, *or in yourself,* that is a sign that you need to be extra careful to check the facts with a variety of other sources and to find out what the arguments are on the other side of the issue.

Ground Rules for Polemicists

Do unto your own as you do unto others. Apply the same standards to yourself and your allies that you do to your opponents, in all of the following ways.

1. Identify your own ideological viewpoint and how it might bias your arguments. Having done so, show that you approach opponents' actions and writings with an open mind, not with malice aforethought. Concede the other side's valid arguments—preferably toward the beginning of your critique, not tacked on grudgingly at the end or in inconspicuous subordinate clauses. Acknowledge points on which you agree at least partially and might be able to cooperate.
2. Summarize the other side's case fully and fairly, in an account

that they would accept, prior to refuting it. Present it through its most reputable spokespeople and strongest formulations (not through the most outlandish statements of its lunatic fringe), using direct quotes and footnoted sources, not your own, undocumented paraphrases. Allow the most generous interpretation of their statements rather than putting the worst light on them; help them make their arguments stronger when possible.
3. When quoting selected phrases from the other side's texts, accurately summarize the context and tone of the longer passages and full texts in which they appear.
4. When you are repeating a secondhand account of events, say so—do not leave the implication that you were there and are certain of its accuracy. Cite your source and take account of its author's possible biases, especially if the author is your ally.
5. In any account that you use to illustrate the opponents' misbehavior, grant that there may be another side to the story and take pains to find out what it is. If opponents claim they have been misrepresented, give them their say and the benefit of the doubt.
6. Be willing to acknowledge misconduct, errors, and fallacious arguments by your own allies, and try scrupulously to establish an accurate proportion and sense of reciprocity between them and those you criticize in your opponents. Do not play up the other side's forms of power while denying or downplaying your own side's. Do not weigh an ideal, theoretical model of your side's beliefs against the most corrupt actual practices on the other side.
7. Respond forthrightly to opponents' criticisms of your own or your side's previous arguments, without evading key points. Admit it when they make criticisms you cannot refute.
8. Do not substitute ridicule or name-calling for reasoned argument and substantive evidence.

Topics for Discussion and Writing

1. *"In regard to any belief that you are convinced is based on facts or the truth, ask yourself how you came to believe it is true. In other words, what is your viewpoint on it, and how did you acquire that viewpoint? From what sources of information did you get the belief—your family, teachers, peers, church, political leaders, news, entertainment, and advertising media? Others? Where did those sources get their beliefs? What might be the limitations or biases in your knowledge, and in that*

of your sources?" The next time you hear a personal acquaintance (or yourself!) express a strong opinion on a controversial public matter, ask these questions. Report the results to your class.
2. How applicable to today's education and society do you think the quoted passages from Mario Savio's 1964 speech are? In his conclusion, speaking as an activist in the movements for civil rights in the South and campus political organizing, he declared, "But an important minority of men and women coming to the front today have shown that they will die rather than be standardized, replaceable, and irrelevant." Study the rise and decline of campus activism since the 1960s to find possible explanations, and speculate about whether any foreseeable course of events might lead to this kind of passion.
3. Study current political writers, speakers, or media commentators for examples of the patterns in "Rhetoric: A Checklist," "A Semantic Calculator for Bias in Rhetoric," and "Ground Rules for Polemicists."

2

Thinking Critically about Political Rhetoric

Prestudy Exercises

1. How would you define the words *liberal* and *conservative*? Just use free association, without too much deliberation and without looking the words up.
2. How do you think an ardent conservative would define *liberal* and *conservative*? How do you think an ardent liberal would define the same words?
3. Look up the following words in a current collegiate dictionary: *conservative, liberal, libertarian, radical, right wing, left wing, fascism, plutocracy, capitalism, socialism, communism, Marxism, democracy, totalitarianism, freedom, free enterprise*. Only note the definitions pertinent to political ideology, not any other senses.
4. Either individually or in teams of classmates, compare the definitions of some of these terms in (a) two or more current dictionaries, (b) a collegiate-sized dictionary, an abridged dictionary, and (at the library or online) an unabridged dictionary.

POLITICAL SEMANTICS

To begin with, *liberal, conservative,* and other terms like those in the prestudy exercises are constantly used by American politicians, mass media, and individuals as though they had a fixed, universally agreed-upon definition; yet, as these exercises have probably indicated to you, such terms are almost infinitely ambiguous, especially when writers and speakers fail to indicate the exact sense or context in which they are using the words. Politicians and other public figures sometimes deliberately exploit the ambiguity of these terms by using them simply as **cleans and dirties**, strong on connotative slanting but weak in denotative meaning. Much similar confusion is caused in argumentation when two opponents deliberately or unconsciously use different definitions of these terms as underlying assumptions—that is, they **stack the deck** by using the definitions favorable to their own side and unfavorable to the opponent's. Thus, the conservative is apt to assume a definition of *conservative* something like "cautious, responsible, moral" and of *liberal* something like "wasteful, permissive, immoral," while the liberal uses *liberal* to mean "open-minded, humane, progressive" and *conservative* to mean "bigoted, greedy, and hypocritically self-righteous." (Remember a key axiom of semantics and rhetoric: whoever defines the terms gains the upper hand in argumentation.)

How much help are dictionary definitions of these terms? Here are the pertinent definitions in *Random House Webster's College Dictionary* (2001 edition):

> **liberal**. Favorable to progress or reform, as in political or religious affairs. Pertaining to, based on, or having views or policies advocating individual freedom of action and expression. Of or pertaining to representational forms of government rather than aristocracies and monarchies. Free from prejudice or bigotry; tolerant. Free of or not bound by traditional or conventional ideas, values, etc.; open-minded.
>
> **conservative**. Disposed to preserve existing conditions, institutions, etc., or to restore traditional ones, and to limit change. Cautiously moderate. Traditional in style or manner; avoiding novelty or showiness. Having the power or tendency to conserve.

Now, in some of these senses—such as attitudes toward reform or change—the two ideologies are clearly opposed. But in other senses, the two are incomparable, like apples and oranges. Nothing in the definitions of *conservative,* or in most contemporary American conservatives' professed beliefs, suggests that conservatives want to restore aristocracies and monarchies, that they oppose progress, that they are intolerant or opposed to individual freedom (indeed, many conservatives believe *they* are the defenders of individual freedom against encroachments by liberals). Likewise, few liberals consider themselves incautious or absolutely opposed to tradition and conservation (indeed, contemporary American liberals tend to be more committed to environmental conservation than most conservatives). Moreover, each side regularly accuses the other of **compartmentalized thinking** in pursuing behavior or policies that are just the opposite of their professed ideals.

So not even the largest unabridged dictionary provides an adequate explanation of the context of oppositions between liberals and conservatives, or leftists and rightists, at any particular historical time or place, including present-day America. Fully understanding those oppositions necessitates a far more complex, multidimensional study in semantics. What are some of these dimensions?

LIBERALISM, CONSERVATISM, DEMOCRAT, REPUBLICAN

Within any single ideological belief, there are usually many different varieties, degrees, and factions, all of whom disagree, often heatedly, among themselves, although they are generally united in opposition to broader ideological adversaries. Contemporary American conservatives are divided among numerous factions, "paleoconservative" traditionalists versus neoconservatives (converts from liberalism, maintaining vestiges of liberal ideas but advocating a more aggressive foreign policy), the religious right versus libertarians (there is also, however, a Libertarian Party opposing both Republicans and Democrats), blue-collar and middle-class conservatives (the "Joe the Plumber" stereotype) versus upper-class ones ("country club conservatives"), small businesspeople versus multinational corporate executives and inheritors of fortunes, and so on. Those who call themselves conservative run the gamut from Ku Klux Klanners and American Nazis to upholders of an earlier, patrician notion of conservatism defending hereditary aristocracy, a united church and state, and the elite, high culture of Western civilization.

American liberals likewise are divided among factions, which include, among others, organized labor, the majority of poor people and racial minorities, teachers and scholars (especially in the liberal arts), liberally inclined members of the upper classes ("limousine liberals"), feminists, environmentalists, consumer advocates, and centrist Democrats like Bill and Hillary Clinton. When Barack Obama was elected president in 2008, he appeared to be quite liberal, but throughout his first term, his liberal supporters thought he moved increasingly toward the center or right. This mix is further complicated by the fact that the Democratic Party, which most liberals support, was through the mid-twentieth century the party of very conservative big-city political machines, Southern white segregationists, and "Reagan Democrats" (former rank-and-file Democrats who since the 1960s have became more conservative and in many cases shifted to voting Republican). Increasingly into the twenty-first century, Democratic politicians have been influenced by large corporate campaign contributors and lobbyists similar to those who support the Republicans; in many cases the same ones contribute to and lobby both parties. In addition to "Hollywood liberals," discussed in Chapter 3, there has been a marked shift toward the Democrats among those corporate wealthy who are highly educated entrepreneurs in computer technology or finance, more aligned with Democratic support of higher education and, in their cosmopolitanism, opposed to the increasing influence of social conservatives in the Republican Party. (See David Callahan's *Fortunes of Change: The Rise of the Liberal Rich and the Remaking of America*.)

Because of the influence of the conservative and corporate-liberal factions in the Democratic Party, many people who consider themselves left-of-liberal (most prominently, members of the New Left movements that arose in the 1960s) dissociate themselves from the party or would like to see it move much further to the left than it has been since at least the time of Roosevelt's New Deal in the 1930s and 1940s. So it is a semantic fallacy, which you should avoid, to use *Democrat* and *liberal* synonymously. In other words, an **argument from the converse** must be avoided here: most liberals are Democrats, but most Democrats are not necessarily liberals.

If many Democrats are conservatives, are there also liberal Republicans? Yes, though fewer than conservative Democrats. Before about 1968, there was a sizeable liberal wing of the Republican Party, represented by leaders like Nelson Rockefeller and the young George H. W. Bush. Since the presidencies of Richard Nixon, Ronald Reagan, and the two Bushes, the party has increasingly been dominated by its conservative wing, with an even sharper conservative turn under the recent influence of the Tea Party movement. John McCain in the 2000 primaries positioned himself to the left of George W. Bush, but he moved to the right in the 2008 election. Mitt Romney was relatively liberal in his early career but turned to the right in 2012, though he was still closer to the center than the rest of the Republican candidates that year, who were unusually far to the right. Nevertheless, you should avoid equating *conservative* with *Republican* in opposition to *Democrat,* mainly because of the large numbers of conservative Democrats.

The term *neoliberalism,* which has come into usage in the past few decades, is another source of semantic confusion, since there is little consensus on its definition. One possible way to understand it is as a revival of the eighteenth-century meaning of *liberalism,* referring to unrestricted economic free enterprise. That makes it most similar to contemporary libertarian conservatism, not only in favoring privatization of previously public sectors of the domestic economy (e.g., education) and unrestricted concentration of corporate wealth, but in promoting a global economy that enables corporations to override national boundaries and allegiances in seeking out, in poorer countries, the cheapest labor while avoiding unions, taxes, and environmental regulation. Most leaders of both the Republican and Democratic parties have supported neoliberal policies (e.g., President Clinton and Vice President Gore pushed NAFTA, the North American Free Trade Agreement), but many liberals and leftists (along with Tea Party conservatives) attack neoliberalism as a new form of colonialism and as a means of moving American jobs overseas while driving down domestic wages for the reduced number of jobs left.

The diversity of interests within both major American parties suggests the semantic problems presented by the culturally conditioned assumption of a two-party system, in contrast to the multiparty system of most other contemporary democracies. One wit has observed that if the Democratic Party were in any Western European country, it would be five different parties. The multiplicity of constituencies in both parties, the overlap of some similar constituencies in both parties, and the widespread influence of corporate wealth in both—all diminishing the differences between the two—frequently result in an **either-or** fallacy: many voters, disillusioned with one party, turn toward the other for a while, then when they get disillusioned with that one, turn back toward the first again, without understanding that both are too diffuse and compromised to provide any significant alternative to one another. There *are* other parties on the ballot in many states, such as the Reform Party, the Libertarian Party, the American Independent Party (more consistently conservative than the Republicans), the New Party, Peace and Freedom, and Socialist parties (all pro-labor and democratic socialist), and the Green Party (environmentalist); there is no law preventing voters from turning to them, or to independent candidates like Ralph Nader and Ross Perot. Many political analysts believe that breaking the monopoly of the two-party system, or at least establishing proportional representation in legislatures, which would enable other parties to gain seats in proportion to their votes, would be a progressive step for American politics and clear public discourse.

> *Grammatical Note: In the context of U.S. politics,* Democrat *and* Republican *are the names of parties, and as such must always be capitalized;* liberal *and* conservative *are names of ideologies—that is, systems of political or philosophical beliefs—so they and other ideological terms discussed here subsequently should never be capitalized except at the beginning of sentences. In the United States there is no such thing as "the Liberal Party" or "the Conservative Party."* Democratic *is the adjective form of the party's name;* democratic *is the adjective form for the ideology of democracy. Likewise for* Republican *and* republican. *In other words, most Republicans are democrats and most Democrats are republicans. Although we cannot hear these distinctions in speaking (we have to make them through the context of surrounding words), it can be very confusing for readers if you do not use the correct capitalization in writing.*

SOCIALISM, COMMUNISM, MARXISM

Yet another set of terms that are widely used in a confusing manner includes *socialism, communism,* and *Marxism.* Here again, each of these ideologies contains many opposing variations and factions among its adherents. *Socialism* is the broadest term; *communism* and *Marxism* are two of many varieties, or subsets, of socialism. (See "A Guide to Political Terms and Positions" later in this chapter for further explanation.) Capitalization usage for these terms varies widely among writers and publishers; most commonly, *Socialist* and *Communist* are used in reference to particular political parties, *socialist* and *communist* in reference to the ideologies, the usage I follow in this book.

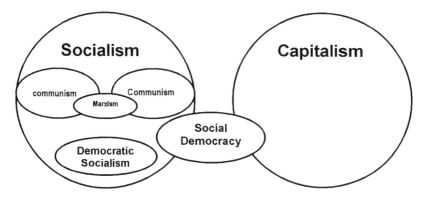

Figure 2.1

Marxism can denote either the theoretical views of Karl Marx and his followers or the political doctrines applied by Communist parties and governments claiming to base their practices on Marxist ideology. The complications here begin with the infinity of disagreements among the intellectual followers of Marxist ideology—the varying degrees of their acceptance of Marx's original views and of revisions of them adjusted to changing historical circumstances from Marx's time, their emphasis on different facets of Marxism, including Marxist philosophy, economics, history, sociology, anthropology, cultural criticism, and so on. Most contemporary Marxist theorists interpret Marxism as a democratic ideology, but the political practice of self-styled Marxist parties and governments (sometimes designated Marxist-Leninist) has most often been undemocratic and totalitarian—causing many theoretical Marxists to denounce Communist parties for exploiting Marx's concept of communism (lowercase *c*) to institute perverse distortions of his ideals. Marxist or neo-Marxist theory has continued to exert a strong influence in the contemporary intellectual and academic world; many scholars who are not doctrinaire Marxists, including myself, have found validity in one form and degree or another of Marxist ideas (again, in support of democracy and freedom); in fact, several of the aspects of critical thinking in this book and chapter reflect Marxist concepts. A common rhetorical tactic of political rightists, however, has been to try to discredit theoretical Marxist scholars and their ideas through red-baiting **guilt by association** with Communist dictatorships. (The circle diagrams, figure 2.1, may help to clarify the relations among these terms.)

THE WORLD POLITICAL SPECTRUM

Terms like *liberal* and *conservative, leftist* and *rightist* are ambiguous not only because they have a vast number of denotations and connotations but also because they cannot be accurately understood in isolation but only within a larger context, framework, or schema of beliefs and relative positions on a spectrum. The writer seeking accuracy of definition needs to key these political terms to a spectrum of positions from far right to far left in the United States and the rest of the world (see table 2.1).

Table 2.1 is based on the world alignment from the time of World War II to around 1990. Much has changed since 1990, rendering some of the schema obsolete; it is also a very broad sketch and does not purport to be all-inclusive. However, this model retains value as a map of the alignments that shaped our concepts of the left and right in world and American politics over most of the twentieth century and that in some important ways persist in the twenty-first. (See the more extensive notes on table 2.1 at the end of this chapter for some of the modifications in the twenty-first century.) Upheavals in the Communist world since the 1980s have especially compounded semantic complexities: the adjective "left-wing" has been historically equated with communism as a political and economic ideology opposed to capitalism, but if left-wing is defined as opposition to the status quo, does that make those who overturned the status quo in Communist countries leftists or rightists? In post–Cold War Eastern Europe, supporters of the old Communist regime are now generally designated "right-wing" and "conservative," while those working for democratic government and a capitalist economy are designated "liberal."

Several further explanations and qualifications are also necessary regarding table 2.1. "Social democratic" is the term applied to the mixed economy in Canada and Western European democracies, which maintain a basically capitalist economy but with considerably more government regulation of business; more progressively structured taxes (i.e., increasing percentage of tax on higher-level incomes); and more government-subsidized health care, higher education, and family benefits. (See Steve Brouwer's "If We Decided to Tax the Rich" at www.paradigmpublishers.com/Books/BookDetail.aspx?productID=321369 as an argument for the benefits of European-style social democracy over American capitalism.) Since the 1980s, Western European countries have moved toward somewhat more privatization in these fields, but still not to the extent of the United States. So a politician or position labeled "moderate" in

Table 2.1. Twentieth-Century Political Spectrum

←——— Left Wing		Right Wing ———→	
Dictatorship	Political Democracy, Freedom		Dictatorship
Communism → Socialism →	Capitalism →		Plutocracy Fascism →

Communism	Socialism	Political Democracy (Socialism)	Capitalism	Plutocracy / Dictatorship	Fascism
USSR	Nicaragua (Sandinista)	Sweden	France		Chile (Pinochet)
China	Chile (Allende)	Denmark	Italy	USA	Philippines (Marcos)
Cuba		Norway	Germany	Japan	South Africa (Apartheid)
North Vietnam			Spain		El Salvador (1980s)
Cambodia			Canada		Nicaragua (Somosa)
North Korea			England		South Vietnam
Zimbabwe					South Korea
					Taiwan
					Indonesia
					Nazi Germany
					Fascist Italy
					Franco Spain
					Fascist Japan

American Parties
Green   Democratic   Republican
Libertarian

the United States is considered right-wing from today's European or Canadian perspective, while many American "radicals" would be "moderates" in Europe or Canada. Similarly, many "ultraconservatives" in American terminology appear "moderate" in comparison to fascistic countries. The practical significance is that, to expose themselves to a fuller range of ideological viewpoints, students need to seek out sources, mainly left-of-liberal and libertarian, excluded from the mainstream of American discourse, though such sources may be hard to find in many communities.

Another semantic confusion in American public discourse results from our tendency to equate terms referring to governmental systems, such as *democracy, freedom,* and *dictatorship,* with words referring to economic systems—*capitalism* or *free enterprise* and *socialism.* As indicated in the bracketed terms in table 2.1 and in the Guide to Political Terms below, in dictionary definitions and in actual historical practice, both a capitalist and a socialist economy can exist under either a democratic or dictatorial government. To oversimplify a complex point, capitalism under a political dictatorship is plutocracy, socialism under a political dictatorship is (capital C) Communism, while fascism consists of a combination of socialist and capitalist economies in the service of militaristic nationalism, as opposed to the internationalistic essence of socialism in general (*Nazi* is an acronym of *National Socialist*), under an all-powerful political dictatorship.

One must again go beyond dictionary definitions to address the relation between these political and economic systems in actual practice, for partisans of varying ideologies assume different connections between, say, freedom and democracy on one hand and capitalism and socialism on the other. Conservatives argue that capitalistic free enterprise is the economic system that best contributes to political freedom and democracy, but leftists argue (as in the socialist position described in the Guide to Political Terms below) that free enterprise in practice tends to destroy democracy and freedom because capitalists gain excessive political power. To the extent that in American usage *capitalism* is commonly used synonymously with political democracy and freedom—in disregard of the dictionary definitions—conservatives have managed to control the semantic agenda, excluding from public discourse widespread arguments for democratic socialism or social democracy. If conservatives say, for example, "Post-Communist Russia moved toward democracy," when the fact is that Russia moved toward a capitalist economy, this argument is based on the underlying assumption that capitalism necessarily leads to democracy. Leftists would refute this argument somewhat as follows: "Russia's turn toward capitalism does not necessarily mean a turn toward democracy; a political dictatorship of the Communist Party is simply being replaced by a political dictatorship of capitalists." More generally, leftists argue, "Sweden, Norway, and Denmark—with semisocialistic economies—certainly have more democratic politics than many capitalist countries like pre-Castro Cuba, El Salvador in the 1980s, South Africa before free elections there, the Philippines under Marcos, or Indonesia and Saudi Arabia today—all dictatorships supported by the United States because they were friendly to American business and military interests. Furthermore, the United States has befriended China, not because it has changed into a democracy, but because it has changed from a Communist dictatorship into a capitalist dictatorship, which provides cheap labor for American corporations and trillions of dollars in American government and business loans. The United States usually gets along fine with dictatorships, so long as they are capitalist and do business with American corporations."

THE AMERICAN POLITICAL SPECTRUM

Looking at the placement of American parties in the worldwide left-to-right spectrum in table 2.1 calls attention to the ethnocentrically limited span of ideology represented by the poles of the Republican and Democratic parties and of "conservatism" and "liberalism" that define the boundaries of most American political, journalistic, scholarly, and cultural discourse. Political forces that are considered liberal in the United States, for example, usually stay well within the limits of capitalist ideology, and thus are considerably to the right of the labor, social-democratic, and Communist parties with large constituencies in most other democratic countries today. We need to keep this limitation in mind when we consider controversies over political viewpoints in American communications media. (Chapter 3 further develops the complexities of this topic.)

As with American political figures, the whole range of American news media—along with individual journalists and scholars, and even figures or shows in popular entertainment like Mel Gibson and George Clooney, Doonesbury and Mallard Fillmore, *The Apprentice* and *The Simpsons*—can be placed on a spectrum from left to right in such a precise way that their political identity can be agreed on to a large extent by those of every ideological persuasion. In both sections of table 2.2, even the division into columns is an arbitrary semantic oversimplification of what could be broken down into several more columns or even a continuous, linear spectrum from left to right.

Table 2.2 American Media, Journalists, and Commentators from Left to Right

A. Media

1. Left	2. Liberal	3. Liberal-to-Conservative	4. Conservative
The Nation	*NY Review*	*Time*	*Reader's Digest*
In These Times	*Harper's*	*Newsweek*	*Weekly Standard*
Mother Jones	*New Yorker*	CNN	*Wall St. Journal*
Extra!	PBS Documentaries	*Washington Post*	*Commentary*
The Progressive	60 Minutes	*Atlantic*	*American Spectator*
Z Magazine	*New York Times*	*New Republic*	*National Review*
Media Matters	MSNBC	*Reason*	Fox News
Pacifica Radio		CBS news	*Washington Times*
American Prospect		NBC, ABC news	*Insight*
		PBS News Hour	Most local newspapers, TV & radio

B. Journalists and Commentators

1. Left	2. Liberal	3. Libertarian	4. Conservative
Noam Chomsky	Jim Lehrer	Virginia Postrel	Rush Limbaugh
Edward Herman	Oprah Winfrey	Stephen Moore	Pat Buchanan
Katrina vanden Heuvel	Rosie O'Donnell	Doug Bandow	Pat Robertson
Barbara Ehrenreich	Bob Woodward	Debra Saunders	David Brooks
Robert Scheer	Mark Shields	Nat Hentoff	Sam Donaldson
Jonathan Kozol	Paul Krugman	James Pinkerton	George Will
Jim Hightower	Stephen Colbert	Jesse Ventura	John McLaughlin
Bob Herbert	Michael Kinsley	Ron Paul	Fred Barnes
Jeff Cohen	Frank Rich	Nick Gillespie	Paul Gigot
Norman Solomon	Gloria Steinem	P. J. O'Rourke	Charles Krauthammer
Victor Navasky	Seymour Hersh		Jonah Goldberg
Roger Wilkins	Carl Bernstein		Phyllis Schlafly
Cornel West	Donald Barlett		John Leo
Ralph Nader	James Steele		Cal Thomas
Katha Pollit	Naomi Wolf		Thomas Sowell
Jesse Jackson	Jon Stewart		Gordon Liddy
Bernie Sanders	James Carville		Bob Grant
Michael Moore	George Stephanopolous		Don Imus
Eric Alterman	Cynthia Tucker		R. Emmett Tyrrell
Lewis Lapham	Al Franken		Laura Ingraham
William Greider	Bill Maher		Mona Charen
Barbara Kingsolver	Keith Olbermann		William Kristol
Arundhati Roy	Eugene Robinson		Sean Hannity
Bill Moyers	Al Sharpton		Rich Lowry
Holly Sklar	Chris Matthews		Norman Podhoretz
Amy Goodman	Julianne Malveaux		John Podhoretz
Thomas Frank	Ezra Klein		Matt Drudge
Chris Hedges	David Cay Johnston		Dinesh D'Souza
Rachel Maddow	Jonathan Chait		Liz Cheney
David Corn	Jane Mayer		Florence King
Melissa Harris-Perry	Arianna Huffington*		Mary Matalin
Chris Hayes	David Brock*		Christina Sommers
Ed Schultz	Michael Lind*		Ann Coulter
Matt Taibbi			Jeff Jacoby
John Nichols			Tucker Carlson
David Sirotta			Bill O'Reilly
			Bernard Goldberg
			Michael Savage
			Michelle Malkin
			Grover Norquist
			Jennifer Rubin
			Joe Scarborough
			David Horowitz*

*Former conservative   *Former leftist

Rather than speak of "the liberal *New York Times,*" one should explain and document the sense and degree of liberalism referred to. "Liberal" in relation to what other media? One might clarify the label by placing the *Times* to the left of *Time* but to the right of *The Nation.* (Many of these placements are disputable, to be sure, and subject to revision as different media and individuals periodically shift their positions. The placement of libertarians is especially problematic; here they are placed between liberal and conservative, but for more refinement, see the following Guide to Political Terms and Positions.)

A GUIDE TO POLITICAL TERMS AND POSITIONS

Left Wing, Right Wing, Capitalism, Communism, Socialism

After we establish a spectrum of positions from far left to far right, we still need to concretize the notions of left and right in terms of specific ideological beliefs, as follows.

Left wing and right wing (also see table 2.1). *The left wing* (adjective: *left-wing* or *leftist*) is a broad term that includes a diversity of parties and ideologies (which often disagree among themselves but usually agree in their opposition to the right wing) including liberals, nearest the center of the spectrum, and—progressively toward the left—socialists and communists (the latter two are also sometimes called "radical"). *Progressive* is a word that is sometimes used synonymously with *liberal* but is sometimes a euphemism for a more radical leftist.

The right wing (adjective: *right-wing* or *rightist*) is a broad term that includes a diversity of parties and ideologies (which often disagree among themselves but usually agree in their opposition to the left wing) including libertarians, nearest the center of the spectrum, and—progressively toward the right—conservatives, ultraconservatives, plutocrats, and fascists.

Leftists tend to support	*Rightists tend to support*
The poor and working class	Middle and upper class
Labor (employees), consumers, environmental and other regulation of business	Management (employers), business, unregulated enterprise

More equality (economic, racial, sexual) than at present	The present state of equality, or return to earlier states
Civil and personal liberties; government control over economic liberty	Economic liberty; controls on personal liberties (e.g., abortion, prayer in schools, sexual conduct)
Cooperation	Competition
Internationalism	Nationalism (primary loyalty to one's own country)
Pacifism (exception: Communists)	Strong military and willingness to go to war
Questioning of authority—skepticism (exception: Communism is authoritarian)	Acceptance of authority, especially in military, police, and strong "law and order" policies
Government spending for public services like education, welfare, health care, unemployment insurance, broadcasting	Government spending for military, subsidies to business as incentive for growth and competition against public sector
Progressive taxes, i.e., greatest burden on wealthy individuals and corporations	Low taxes for wealthy individuals and corporations as incentive for investment ("supply-side economics" or "trickle-down theory")
Religious pluralism, skepticism, or atheism	Religious orthodoxy

Capitalism. Capitalism is an economic system based on private investment for profit. Jobs and public services are provided, and public needs met, to the extent that investment in them will predictably result in a return of capital outlay. In its principles capitalism does not provide any restrictions on extremes of wealth and poverty or on social power, but its advocates (especially pure, libertarian capitalists) believe that the workings of a free-market economy, unrestricted by government controls or regulation, will minimize social inequity.

Capitalism is not a political system; in principle, a capitalist economy can operate under either a democratic government or a dictatorship, as in plutocracy or fascism (see table 2.1).

Socialism. An economic system based on public investment to meet public needs, provide full employment, and reduce socioeconomic inequality. Socialism does not allow great extremes of wealth and poverty, though most forms allow for some range of differences in salary. In various models of socialism, investment and industrial management are controlled either by the federal government or by local governments, workers' and consumers' cooperatives, a variety of community groups, and so on. Socialism is not a political system; in principle, a socialist economy can operate under either a democratic government or a dictatorship, as in Communism (see table 2.1).

Communism. With lowercase c, communism refers to Marx's ideal of the ultimate, future form of pure democratic socialism, with virtually no need for centralized government. With uppercase C as in present-day Communist parties, Communism is a socialist economy under undemocratic government. Historically, Communists have manipulated appeals to left-wing values like socioeconomic equality and worldwide cooperation in order to impose police-state dictatorship and military aggression.

Plutocracy. Rule by the rich; a capitalist economy under undemocratic government.

Fascism. A combination of capitalist and socialist economies under an undemocratic government. Historically, fascists have manipulated appeals to conservative values like patriotism, religion, competitiveness, anticommunism, respect for authority and law and order, traditional morality and the family, in order to impose police-state dictatorship. Fascism typically is aggressively militaristic and imperialistic and promotes racial hatred based on theories of white (or "pure Aryan") supremacy and religious persecution of non-Christians. It glorifies strong authority figures with absolute power.

Conservatives, Liberals, Socialists, Libertarians

Conservatives. In the American context, most conservatives are pro-capitalist, believing that a capitalist economy best promotes political democracy. In other words, they believe what's profitable for big business also serves the interests of good government, labor, consumers, the environment, and the public in general—"What's good for General Motors is good for America." As conservative journalist David Horowitz asserts, "Entrepreneurs generally want a better-educated, better-paid, more diverse working force, because that means better employees, better marketers, and better consumers of the company product. That is why, historically, everywhere capitalism has been embraced, labor conditions have improved and inequalities have diminished whether there has been a strong trade union presence or not" ("Intellectual Class War"). Because mainstream conservatives believe a major function of government is to help business maximize profits, they justify low taxes and government subsidies, protections, and bailouts for big business such as those for the mortgage industry in 2008–2009 (although libertarian conservatives preferred to let the free market sort out the problems of individuals losing their houses to foreclosures, and irresponsible mortgage lenders bankrupting their companies and causing bond markets to plunge when the housing "bubble" of previous decades burst). They believe that the capitalistic, or free-enterprise, system is the best guarantee of equal social opportunity for everyone and that a large diversity of private enterprises is the best guarantee against excessive concentration of power in government (the main danger of socialism). They believe that abuses by businesses can and should be best policed or regulated by business itself, and when conservatives control government they routinely appoint businesspeople to public administrative positions and regulatory agencies because of their managerial expertise (a practice that liberals view as often leading to conflicts of interest). Mainstream conservatives tend, however, to want government to control *personal* conduct in areas like abortion, censorship, sexual behavior, and religion, with the exception that they oppose gun control.

Liberals. Most American liberals, like conservatives, basically believe in capitalism. But they also believe that the interests of big business are frequently contrary to those of democratic government and of employees, consumers, the environment, and the public in general. They think that capitalism tends to lead to excessive concentration of wealth in a few corporations and individuals, leading in turn toward plutocratic government—dictatorship of the rich. So they think that capitalism needs to be saved from its own self-destructive tendencies and kept on an even keel by policing business abuses through government regulation, by limiting extremes of wealth and poverty through progressive taxation and through welfare, unemployment insurance, Social Security, public education, and other free or low-cost public services. Though they are not "anti-business," as conservatives charge, liberals support labor unions as a counterbalance to the power of big business, and they believe that excessive cutbacks in regulatory agencies pushed through by corporate lobbies beginning with President Reagan's administration have resulted in a drastically accelerating "wealth gap" and several waves of financial scandals and crises. These include the collapse of savings and loan banks in the eighties and of Enron and several other giant corporations in the early 2000s, as well as the crisis in the banking and loan industries, in which top executives pocketed millions while their companies went bankrupt, along with uncontrolled executive salaries and speculative fortunes on Wall Street from arcane investments like hedge funds and derivatives. As noted above, these are the classic positions of the Democratic Party, though that party has moved more in the direction of conservatism in many ways through the last three or four decades. Liberals generally think, however, that government should *not* control personal conduct (except for gun control, which they tend to favor); in this area, they are much the same as libertarians.

Socialists. While liberals (and Democrats) want to save capitalism by regulating it, socialists want to replace it altogether. And while American liberals support the Democratic Party, socialists see both Democrats and Republicans as pro-capitalist, plutocratic parties, so they favor forming separate socialist or labor parties. American socialists, or radicals, believe more strongly than liberals that the interests of big business are contrary to democracy and the public interest; they believe that capitalism is basically an irrational, corrupt system; that the profit motive is destructive of the natural environment, public health and safety, and traditional morality; and that wealthy business interests inevitably gain control over government, foreign and military policy, the media, and education and use the power of employment to keep the workforce and electorate under their control. They believe it is in the nature of capitalism for many (not all) owners of businesses to maximize profits by charging customers "whatever the traffic will bear" and by getting the most work out of employees for the lowest wages and cheapest working conditions possible. Socialists view globalization as a strategy by businesses to exploit slave labor abroad and drive down wages for American workers who are in a weakened position to bargain. They think liberal government reforms and attempts to regulate business are usually squashed by the power of business lobbies and that even sincere liberal reformers in government offices usually come from or eventually adopt the ethnocentric viewpoint of the upper classes. The socialist economic alternative is to operate on a nonprofit basis at least the biggest national and international corporations, as well as the defense industry, thereby preventing at the source the excessive accumulation of wealth and power through profits gained by capitalist investors. Socialists also go beyond liberal support of labor unions; they would have most businesses owned and managed democratically by their workers. In other words, socialism is an extension of the principles of democratic government into control of *economic* institutions. On the principle that there are many more workers than capitalists, and that it is the workers whose labor produces the profits that go into capitalists' pockets, a government and economy controlled by the totality of workers would be far more democratic than our present plutocracy. Short of the distant goal of full socialism, they tend (as in Europe and elsewhere) to form "social democratic" parties implementing a "mixed economy" of capitalism and socialism under democratic government, but they move further toward socialism than American liberals and Democrats. Socialists tend to side with liberals and libertarians in not wanting government to control personal conduct (though Communist governments tend to be highly "conservative" in legislating morality).

Libertarians. Libertarians agree with democratic leftists in supporting civil liberties and personal freedom in moral conduct, and with democratic rightists in supporting economic free enterprise with no or minimal government interference, and they accuse both leftists and conservatives of compartmentalized thinking or inconsistencies between the two realms. Thus, while libertarianism is one form of conservatism, libertarians criticize mainstream conservatives for inconsistency when they support government subsidies or bailouts for business or protectionist policies supposedly in the national interest. They are neither nationalistic and militaristic (like mainstream conservatives) nor for international cooperation (like leftists); they believe in unrestricted economic competition and free trade internationally as the best road to world peace. They oppose military drafts and favor minimal government spending on defense. They tend to oppose big defense spending as a racket for special interests and agree with leftists that arms races and wars result from excessive influence of the military and the defense industry on the government and economy of each opposing country.

NOTES ON THE GUIDE TO POLITICAL TERMS AND POSITIONS

I have attempted here to arrive at definitions that are acceptable to leftists and rightists alike—or at least to arrive at agreement between leftists and rightists on what they disagree about. This is a fiendishly difficult enterprise, since it is nearly inevitable that anyone attempting to do this, even with the best intentions, will stack the deck to some extent by projecting her or his own biases into the definitions. The best way to deal with this difficulty is to get suggestions for improvements from people on the other side, as I have done in modifying this schema over several years. The whole schema is best understood as an exercise in semantic open-endedness, open to constant, dialogic revision; you should use it that way too, adding your own and your classmates' suggestions for improvement.

A Note on Leftists and Rightists

The topics under "Leftists tend to support" and "Rightists tend to support" need much qualification. Note the phrasing "tend to"; that is to say, these oppositions and other general categories in this section are not asserted as absolute or total but only indicate the sympathies of the majority of people in each group, taking account of many exceptions and historical changes of allegiance. As for the list of issues on which leftists and rightists are opposed, there is bound to be dispute over the very way these oppositions are set up. For example, as the summary of the conservative position above indicates, conservatives will argue that the interests of the wealthy, business, management, and unregulated enterprise are not opposed to the interests of the poor, working class, employees, consumers, or the environment. Their arguments may be persuasive, yet the neutral fact remains that leftists and rightists constantly argue over whether these sets of interests are opposed or not.

Also note that the first oppositions in the two columns describe what groups those on opposing sides *support,* not what ones they themselves belong to. For instance, are all upper-class individuals or corporate executives in America right-wing and Republican? By no means. The Democratic Party has always had a wealthy contingent in its leadership ranks, though less so than the Republicans, who have long been identified as the business party. In the past few decades, an increasing number of rich people and corporation executives, especially those with higher levels of education, have switched to the Democrats for a variety of reasons. Most intellectuals, scientists, and artists are Democrats, and Republicans have increasingly become characterized by populist anti-intellectualism, waging a culture war against alleged artistic licentiousness and academic liberal elitism, and by rejection of mainstream science in issues like evolution and climate change. Republicans have supported Reaganomics or supply-side economics, which is rejected by most academic economists. Many among the new generation of computer-science billionaires like Bill Gates, Steve Jobs, Mark Zuckerberg, and executives of hedge and equity funds based on advanced mathematics were "nerds" as students, thus trending Democratic.

But, as previously emphasized, not all Democrats are liberals, and most of them certainly are not leftists. So aside from party allegiance, why would any wealthy capitalist embrace liberal or left political beliefs critical of capitalism or leaning toward socialism? Many rich people (prototypically of the Hollywood, limousine liberal variety) are quite liberal on social issues like religion, abortion, sexual conduct, and legalizing drugs, though not so much on economic issues like income inequality, labor unions, and government regulation of business. However, some current super-rich capitalists, like George Soros and Warren Buffet, support liberal economic policies as more conducive to long-run social stability, even though conservative policies like low taxes and reduced regulation may increase their personal, short-term profits. They are still far, however, from supporting socialistic divestment of all wealth or appropriation of corporate ownership and management by workers or government. Liberals consider these figures' support of policies contrary to their financial interests as proof that they are motivated by moral principle rather than selfishness. Liberals likewise consider the large amount of financial support for liberal causes by a prominent figure like Soros as motivated by selfless philanthropy, in contrast to the support by wealthy conservatives like David and Charles Koch of conservative causes such as the Tea Party, causes that advance not only their libertarian ideological principles but their own corporate power and profits. But conservatives like Glenn Beck have accused Soros and other rich liberals of being motivated by lust for power in the Democratic Party, liberal constituencies, and the global economy.

The issues of economic, racial, and sexual equality are among the most heated sources of contemporary disputes. My initial wording here was that leftists tend to support equality and rightists inequality in these areas. My justification was that throughout most of Western history, conservatives have defended undemocratic, established hierarchies of class, race, and gender, while the eighteenth-century movement for democracy that culminated in the American Revolution and the credo that "all men are created equal" (with the significant exception of women and slaves) was the basis of modern liberalism. Even in contemporary America, some conservatives continue to defend certain forms of inequality within a democracy. For example, in *Giants and Dwarfs,* a sequel to his controversial 1987 book *The Closing of the American Mind,* Allan Bloom argues against the excessive democratization of higher education: "The university is, willy-nilly, in some sense aristocratic in both the conventional and natural senses of the term. It cannot, within broad limits, avoid being somewhat more accessible to the children of parents of means than to the children of the poor" (291). And he asserts that the liberal campaign for affirmative action "will brook no vestige of differentiation in qualities between men and women.... It would more willingly accept a totalitarian regime than a free one in which the advantages of money, position, education, and even talent are unevenly distributed" (367). Another way of putting Bloom's argument is that excessive liberal demands for greater equality will have the ironic opposite effect of establishing a new, worse hierarchy of inequality with bureaucratic administrators at its top.

Not all contemporary conservatives go so far in defense of inequality as Bloom, however. A more typical current conservative, or libertarian, line of argument is that unrestricted free enterprise is a more effective means of reducing all forms of inequality than liberal government legislation for affirmative action or progressive taxation, minimum-wage laws, and other attempts at more equitable income distribution. Another line used by conservatives is that they believe in equality of opportunity, as opposed to leftists' belief in equality of outcome, as in affirmative action. Many leftists, however, consider this a false dichotomy, since their position is that minorities, women, and the poor do *not* have equality of opportunity at present, so that affirmative action and other liberal policies are aimed at overcoming *this* inequality, not at attaining rigid equality of outcome. These are the reasons I have revised my wording to define the opposition as one between liberal calls for greater equality than at present versus conservative defenses of our present system as the best guarantor of equality. I hope, again, that this wording allows leftists and rightists to agree on what they disagree on. Do *you* agree, and if not, how can you improve on the definition?

On controversies like abortion, sexual conduct, pornography, legalization of drugs, and prayer in schools, leftists try to control the agenda by defining these issues in terms of civil and personal liberties, while rightists try to define them in terms of conservative morality versus liberal immorality or permissiveness. On morality in general, conservatives accuse leftists of favoring total relativism, hedonism, and rewarding of laziness, in opposition to conservative restraint and industriousness. Leftists claim this is another false dichotomy and **oversimplification**, misrepresenting what they actually believe and involving **selective vision** in ignoring comparable immoral behavior on the part of many conservatives who do not practice what they preach. Since neither side accepts the premises of the other on these issues, no common ground may be attainable here beyond agreement on what the disagreements are.

Another approach to these issues involves the possibility of compartmentalized thinking on both sides. Leftists tend to justify a permissive position on issues of personal morality as a defense of individual liberties against intrusive government control, but on economic issues they favor government control to curb immoral business practices or economic policies that result in excessive wealth and power for the corporate elite. Rightists tend to favor just the opposite: government control over personal morality but not over business morality. Similarly, conservatives say that they oppose big government spending and fostering of individual dependency on government handouts; yet liberals respond that conservatives are all for big government spending and handouts as long as they go to favored conservative constituencies like the military and corporate subsidies or bailouts. Libertarians believe that theirs is the only consistent position on all these issues. Do you agree with them, or can you find statements by either leftists or rightists that reconcile their apparent inconsistencies?

Concerning views on religion, some refinement is needed of the suggestion that leftists favor pluralism, skepticism, or atheism, while rightists favor religious orthodoxy. Certainly it is true that historically liberals, socialists, and communists have tended strongly toward religious skepticism, and consequently toward tolerance of diverse beliefs and even of atheism; at the extreme left, to be sure, Communist governments have been intolerant of religion. But these tendencies on the right and left must be qualified by noting that Protestants, Catholics, Jews, Muslims, and others are all internally divided between conservative and liberal factions; many Catholic "liberation theologians" even have Marxist social sympathies, in spite of Marxism's historical hostility toward religion as "the opiate of the masses." Also, leftists frequently are less opposed to religion itself than to the hypocrisy they claim to find in conservatives who do not practice the religious values they preach. As for conservatives, they might say the word *orthodoxy* has a negative connotation and prefer to replace it with something like "traditional religious beliefs and moral values." Religious conservatives too are divided between evangelical Christians and more ecumenical or pluralistic faiths.

A Note on Fascism

As a consequence of some forty-five years of Cold War anti-Communism (1945–1990), most Americans are probably familiar with the notion that if leftist or even liberal values are pushed to extremes, they can lead toward Communism. Far fewer Americans understand that if conservative values are pushed to extremes, they can lead toward fascism. However, many conservative polemicists do not acknowledge that fascism is conservative; they try to equate fascism with the extreme left ideology of Communism, mainly by stressing that the word *Nazi* in German was an acronym for "National Socialist." As noted earlier, a fascist economy combines socialistic and capitalistic elements toward an all-powerful central government that in some ways *is* quite close to Communist rule. But this line of argument downplays the conservative elements in fascism, including strong nationalism and imperialism (as opposed to socialist internationalism), glorification of military and police strength, subservience to social hierarchies, "pure Aryan" racism, and orthodox religion, family structure, and gender roles (in contrast to Communism's atheism, subordination of the family, and avowed equality for women).

Our concept of fascism is generally limited to movies about Nazi military conquest and atrocities in World War II, which convey little sense of the ideology of fascism. In fact, it might be said that the greatest danger of fascism is that so few people understand what it really is, so many might be attracted to its publicly stated beliefs without comprehending its evils. Several of my students have said, in effect, "Fascism values patriotism, military strength, and obedience to leaders, as well as religious orthodoxy, family values, and law and order. Sounds pretty good to me." What they do not understand is that historically, fascists have manipulated these appeals to gain power and then abolished democracy and imposed brutal dictatorships. Nor did fascism disappear after World War II, as is widely believed; quasi-fascist dictatorships have thrived all around the world up to the present, as indicated in the "Right Wing" column of table 2.1, and the United States has had an embarrassing record of supporting them, partly because they were strongly anti-Communist but also partly because they tended to do business with American corporations and the military.

Fascism is the ultimate manifestation of the human tendency toward authoritarianism and conformity. The "good German" soldiers and civilians under Hitler rationalized going along with Nazi atrocities because "our leader must know what he's doing," and they had been culturally conditioned to obey those in authority. The appeal of fascism is especially strong in periods of national danger, when **appeals to fear** are predictably manipulated by those in power.

Table 2.3 Social Class and Political Attitudes, Left to Right

(These are very general approximations, indicating simply the tendencies of the majority of people in each group, with exceptions, and open to dispute)

LIBERAL   CONSERVATIVE

UPPER CLASS
Income Over $200,000, Net Worth over $5 Million

Limousine Liberals:
   Some Democratic politicians, bureaucrats
   Some executives and "stars" in media
   A few labor union officials

Country Club Conservatives:
   Big business executives and major
     stockholders, corporate lawyers and
     lobbyists

Media owners and advertisers
Top Republican and many Democratic
   politicians
Military top ranks
Top university administrators and trustees

MIDDLE CLASS
Income $30,000-$200,000, Net Worth $100,000-$5 Million

Professors and teachers in liberal arts
Rank and file public employees
Journalists & media employees
Artists
Middle-class minorities
College liberal arts students and graduates

Teachers in business and vocational ed
Independent businesspeople and professionals
White collar employees in the private sector

Vocational college students and grads

WORKING CLASS
Income under $10,000-$30,000, Net worth: Zero to $100,000

Left-wing populists:
   Labor union members
   "Underclass" whites and minorities
     (Income under $15,000, net worth
     under $50,000)

Right-wing populists:
   White race, blue collar, and some white
     collar workers,
   Military rank and file

Notes on Social Class and Political Attitudes

The table on what leftists and rightists tend to support includes "the poor and working class" on the left and "middle and upper class" on the right. These class labels are among the most ambiguous in political usage in this country, where nearly all people tend to describe themselves as middle class and where the even vaguer term "working Americans" serves to blur any distinction between the working and middle class. Up until the mid-twentieth century, "working class" generally meant poor people, blue-collar workers, and those with a high school or lower level of education. The Democratic Party was known as the party of the working class, and the Republicans as the party of the middle class, the rich, and big business. For various historical reasons, these identifications have changed since the 1950s, with the Republicans gaining the allegiance of many at the lower socioeconomic levels and trying to tar the Democrats as the party of "elitism." In the 2008 election campaign, the declining economic situation of most Americans except for the rich prompted Democrats to renew their avowed support for "the working class"—used as a blanket term for everyone in the middle class and below.

Also, as noted earlier, the class people *support* is not always the same class to which they *belong*. Many working-class Americans staunchly defend the rich and are driven by the conservative dream of someday becoming rich themselves. Conversely, conservative pundits ridicule upper-class "limousine liberals" who express concern for the poor and working class. Table 2.3 suggests a very rough, unscientific approximation of the makeup of American social classes and how the classes relate to political attitudes. You can test this schema against your own impressions. The totality of citizens who are termed "liberals" or "conservatives" is a coalition of the very different constituencies belonging to the three socioeconomic classes in the two columns. Most published sources (politicians, journalists, scholars) that you will encounter belong to the upper-middle or upper classes on either the left or right; typically, however, they will claim to be speaking and acting as populists, in support of the lower classes, who lack access to media of public opinion. In predictable rhetorical patterns, those at the upper levels on one side will say that they are true populists, having the interests of the lower levels on their side at heart, while partisans of the other side will accuse those on the first side of being elitists who hypocritically pretend to be populists, manipulating the lower-class masses for their own benefit. So you need to make a judgment call about which side is sincere.

The line suggesting an S-curve from bottom to top indicates the following. In America and other societies, people at the poorest level, left-wing populism, tend to be liberal or leftist, as do those a step above them economically who are unionized workers—labor unions being the prime constituency of the liberal wing of the Democratic Party. (This group also tends to include first-generation immigrants and city dwellers.) People reaching a higher level within the working class, and in sectors like the military, tend more to be conservative Republicans, the constituency of right-wing populism. (This group also includes many rural and small-town dwellers and second-generation immigrants.) These are some of the divisions that after the 2000 presidential election came to identify "Blue States" as Democratic and "Red States" as Republican, although liberal versus conservative attitudes on religion and other "social issues" within this broad socioeconomic range are another complicating variable.

As working-class people, or their children, move up into the middle class and go to college, those who follow business-oriented majors tend to stay on the right through life, while liberal-education majors are more inclined to become liberals, remaining so if they go to work in the public, nonprofit sector (especially teachers and professors) or in media, the arts, and other intellectual fields. If they advance toward upper-class status, those who remain liberal as labor-union or Democratic Party officials, media executives, or "stars" are often termed "limousine liberals" (think Sean Penn, Rosie O'Donnell, and Oprah Winfrey), implying a compartmentalization between class status and political attitudes. It is, however, less common for those who attain this level to remain liberal (which is why the concept of the limousine liberal is something of a paradox) than to swing back toward the right, the natural tendency, almost by definition, of people who attain status, wealth, and power—as, for example, teachers or college faculty who become administrators, journalists who become editors, and performers who become executives.

PREDICTABLE PATTERNS OF POLITICAL RHETORIC

The following list of predictable patterns, like the "Semantic Calculator for Bias in Rhetoric" in Chapter 1, is intended mainly to enable you to recognize a particular line of argument when you see it, not automatically to dismiss it as biased. It is a necessary and perfectly legitimate part of argumentation to make the strongest case you can for your own cause and to point out the faults in opponents' positions. Once you recognize these patterns, the more important task is to evaluate whether the points being played up and downplayed are well-reasoned and supported, or whether they are just appealing one-sidedly to knee-jerk emotional response.

Leftists will play up	*Rightists will play up*
Right-wing bias in media and education; power of business interests and administrators	Left-wing bias in media and education; power of employees and unions

Crimes and fraud by the rich; luxury, waste, selfish interests, and control of government by private industry and the military	Crime and fraud by the poor; luxury and waste by government bureaucrats; selfish interests and control over government by labor unions, teachers, environmentalist and civil rights organizations
Conservative ethnocentrism and sentimentality toward the middle and upper classes and America abroad	Leftist "negative thinking," "sour grapes," anti-Americanism, and sentimentality toward the lower classes and Third World peoples
U.S. military strengths, right-wing "hawks" scare tactics about foreign adversaries' strengths and menace	Foreign adversaries' strengths, menace, and manipulation of left-wing "doves"; left-wing scare tactics about negative consequences of American military actions
Conservative rationalization of right-wing extremism and foreign dictatorships allied with the United States (e.g., South Vietnam in the Vietnam War, El Salvador in the 1980s, Saudi Arabia)	Liberal rationalization of left-wing extremism and Communist dictatorships or guerillas (e.g., Cuba, Sandinista Nicaragua, North Vietnam, Aristide in Haiti, Mugabe in Zimbabwe)

A NOTE ON TWENTY-FIRST-CENTURY MODIFICATIONS TO TABLE 2.1

The worldwide, political spectrum in table 2.1, which goes back to the twentieth-century foundation for the left-to-right spectrum, has undergone considerable change, and as noted earlier, does not aim to be all-inclusive. The major change since the 1990s has been the collapse of the Soviet Union and its satellite Communist governments in Eastern Europe. At this writing, there still exist some Communist dictatorships on the far left (most prominently Cuba, North Korea, Vietnam, and China, though the latter two have moved toward a capitalist economy while remaining political dictatorships) and some semi-fascistic or plutocratic dictatorships on the far right such as Saudi Arabia, Indonesia, and Guatemala, or military dictatorships like Pakistan and Myanmar (Burma). The year 2011 was marked by "the Arab spring," in which masses in Egypt, Syria, Libya, and elsewhere in the Middle East rose up against long-entrenched dictatorships whose oil-rich rulers were American allies, though in some cases they had also appealed to leftist Arab nationalism and anti-colonialism.

However, the extreme poles of Communism on the left and fascism on the right no longer dominate world politics as they did through much of the twentieth century. The United States still remains to the right of Europe, Canada, and Japan on the spectrum of socialist-to-capitalist democracies, although Western Europe in recent decades has seen a resurgence of an extreme right wing, prompted mainly by opposition to swelling ranks of immigrant labor, mostly Arab, which is perceived as a threat to native employment and culture and as a possible source of terrorism. Anti-Semitism is also prevalent in the European right, a phenomenon of compartmentalized thinking, in light of the right's equal anti-Arab bias and of the antagonism between Arabs and Jews in Israel.

Two primary complications have made the worldwide left-right polarity somewhat obsolete, although it remains viable in the American spectrum in table 2.2. One is globalization, which has allowed corporations to a large extent to override nations as economic entities. Advocates of the global economy tend to be conservatives in the sense that they support multinational corporations, although as noted earlier, they are sometimes termed "neoliberal." Opponents of globalization, generally leftists, say neoliberalism is a code word for allowing corporations free rein to impose a new form of worldwide colonialism and plutocracy calculated to drive down wages, worsen working conditions, and undermine unionized labor.

The other recent complication is the prominence of worldwide religious and ethnic conflicts, especially between, and within, the Western and Muslim worlds. Here distinguishing between left and right gets extremely complicated. Islamic terrorism is an outgrowth of Muslim countries that are internally conflicted between two different forms of conservative politics: either secular, plutocratic (mainly oil-rich) forces—some allied with America and Western Europe, like Saudi Arabia and Kuwait, some hostile, like Iraq under Saddam Hussein—or the fundamentalist Islamic movements in countries like Afghanistan and Iran. Islamic fundamentalists embody a confusing mix (at least in Western terms) of conservative religious opposition to secular society and Westernization, and of support for leftist anti-colonialism and populist Arab nationalism. Almost no figures in American public life endorse terrorism or supported Saddam Hussein, but most conservatives are "hawks" and most liberals "doves" in their degree of support for military and domestic antiterrorist policies. Liberals tend to favor more international diplomacy and policies that address underlying causes of Muslim antagonism toward the United States, while conservatives tend to favor primarily military action.

The Israeli-Palestinian conflict is primarily a struggle over land and sovereignty, not ideology, although it also involves religion and colonialism. Arab countries have been antagonistic toward Israel for expelling millions of native Palestinians, who have been dispersed into refugee camps in the lands bordering Israel, and for suppressing those who have remained. Radical Muslim factions have supported terrorism or military action against Israel, with mutual retaliation being endless. Israel is a liberal social democracy internally, but it has been periodically dominated by governments that are right-wing (and closely allied to American conservatives) in their hard-line policy toward the Palestinian Arabs, in contrast to the Israeli left, which seeks compromise with the Palestinians. For these reasons and others, the Middle East is the source of bitter political polarization in America, with conservatives generally supporting Israel, while liberals and leftists generally support the Palestinians. This is one of those situations that is so inflammatory that it is virtually impossible even to define the opposing forces and issues without injecting partisan opinion. (You are welcome to improve on my account.)

POLITICAL VIEWPOINTS IN SOURCES

Many sources that you will use for college papers have an explicit or implicit political viewpoint. The following discussion considers American periodicals, book publishers, and research institutes identified by political position. For lists with online links to these and other partisan sources, see "Directory of Political Media" at www.paradigmpublishers.com/books/BookDetail.aspx?productID=321369.

General Circulation Periodicals

This is a partial list, mainly of journals of opinion, intended to supplement, not replace, more accessible, mass-circulation newspapers and magazines, most of which have a center-conservative to center-liberal orientation. (These hyphenated terms reflect the discussion of table 2.2 above, suggesting that identifying points on a continuous spectrum from left to right would be more accurate than labels like "liberal" and "conservative." A rough approximation can be achieved by sets of terms like "left-liberal," "center-liberal," "right-liberal," and so on.)

Most of the influential national newspapers—such as the *New York Times,* the *Washington Post,* and the *Los Angeles Times*—attempt to strike a balance between liberal and conservative in their reporting, editorial and op-ed pages, and cultural reviews, although they are generally considered predominantly liberal (except by comparison to the smaller journals of opinion to their left, which delight in trashing the big papers for their relative conservatism). The *Wall Street Journal,* however, is openly conservative, especially in its editorial and op-ed sections. The *Washington Times* was founded in the 1980s by the Reverend Sun Myung Moon as a conservative daily counterpart to the *Washington Post.* Most other newspapers around the country—along with TV and radio stations—tend either to be owned by large local business interests and consequently to represent their conservative politics and that of their corporate advertisers and community peers, or, more recently, to have been bought up by conservative national chains, as documented by Ben H. Bagdikian in *The New Media Monopoly.* In reading newspaper or newsmagazine reviews of books on controversial topics, you should be aware that reviews are likely to be colored by the reviewer's own political viewpoint as well as that of the authors reviewed, and that editors' biases sometimes influence whether they assign a book to a reviewer who is on the same side as the author reviewed or to one on the opposing side. In both reviews and other articles written by either staffers or freelance authors (and sometimes even in letters to the editor), editors are also free to demand revisions and even to rewrite the author's text substantially, with or without permission, so much of what we read, watch, or hear may be filtered through editors' biases.

Journals of Opinion

Most journals of opinion now appear both in print and online, where they are updated more often than in their weekly or monthly print versions. In America and other countries, they have served, throughout their centuries-long history, largely as a voice for the particular political viewpoint of their owners (typically a single individual or family), although that viewpoint might change over the years with changes in owners or in the original owners' views. Two of the best-known for over a century have been *The Nation* and the *New Republic;* the early history of both was radical leftist—until the 1950s they were sometimes aligned with the Communist Party. *The Nation* has remained the best-known left-of-liberal journal (anti-Communistic under publisher Victor Navasky, though its critics still claim to find vestiges of its earlier history), while the *New Republic* under the ownership of Martin Peretz since the 1960s has become conservative on some issues, liberal on others. Other accessible journals on the left-of-liberal side include *Progressive, In These Times, Dissent, Mother Jones, Z Magazine, The American Prospect,* and *Extra!* (published by FAIR, or Fairness and Accuracy in Reporting). The *New Yorker* has wide circulation and its scope is broader than politics, but insofar as it is partially a journal of opinion and reportage, in recent decades it has been consistently mainstream liberal. Two magazines well established in American history back to the mid-nineteenth century are *Harper's* and the *Atlantic Monthly*. Like the *New Yorker,* they have semi-mass circulation and contain a wide variety of articles and fiction, but they have been generally liberal in their politics, though this has shifted with changes in owners and editors; in the last decade or so *Harper's* has been decidedly more liberal than *Atlantic Monthly*.

The best-known conservative journals of opinion since the 1950s have been *Commentary* (which under the editorship of Norman Podhoretz shifted sharply from left to right in the late 1960s, and which currently is edited by his son John) and *National Review,* long owned and edited by William F. Buckley, who also was a prominent spokesperson for the right on public television. With the rise of the conservative "counterintelligentsia" since the 1970s has come a profusion of other conservative journals, including *American Spectator* (which began as a semischolarly, conservative counterpart to the *New York Review,* but which now aims at a broader audience and contains more political exposés, opinion, and invective) and the *Weekly Standard,* funded by Rupert Murdoch until 2009 and edited by William Kristol (who was chief of staff to Vice President Dan Quayle), which serves as the unofficial voice of the Republican Party intelligentsia. *Insight,* the weekly magazine of the *Washington Times,* is available at some newsstands nationally, and a *Washington Times* weekly edition also has national circulation, as does the *Washington Post* weekly. Several publications of the conservative research institutes discussed below began as scholarly journals but are now aimed at a general audience: *American Enterprise* (American Enterprise Institute), *Policy Review* (Heritage Foundation), and the *Cato Journal* (Cato Institute). *Reason* is a widely available libertarian journal.

Publishers of Books and Reports

Most of the major publishers of serious nonfiction and fiction books have no fixed political viewpoint, so they publish a mix of conservative and liberal works. Some of them, however, are predominantly, though not exclusively, conservative—Simon and Schuster, Free Press, Basic Books—and others are predominantly liberal, most notably Random House and its Pantheon division. Several smaller presses publish almost exclusively conservative books and others almost exclusively liberal to left-of-liberal ones.

Research Institutes and Foundations ("Think Tanks")

Most of the American public is not very familiar with the workings of research institutes, also known as "think tanks," or the foundations that fund them, but they have become increasingly influential in the formation of public opinion in the past few decades, along partisan political lines. Throughout the twentieth century and into the twenty-first, large American universities have housed a variety of research institutes where faculty members work virtually full-time rather than teach; teaching faculties also conduct research projects with funding from government agencies, corporations, nonprofit foundations, and occasionally labor or consumer organizations. In both universities and the more recent private research institutes, projects dealing directly or indirectly with socioeconomic or environmental issues may have a liberal or conservative bias according to the researchers' and funders' own ideological inclinations. The best way to find out whether a book or report you use as a source has been sponsored by a foundation or think tank, liberal or conservative, is to look in the acknowledgments section at the beginning or end of most journalistic and scholarly books, where the author will thank such-and-such a foundation or institute for financial support. Think tanks also place newspaper op-eds and magazine articles by their affiliated "fellows," and the affiliations of such writers are typically indicated in a biographical note.

In the early 1970s, a group of national conservative leaders sought a solution to what they saw as the overall liberal or left-of-liberal bias of American universities, at least in the humanities and social sciences, and of the media, foundations, and intellectual life generally. They set out to build up a conservative "counterintelligentsia" by persuading several large corporations and corporate-aligned foundations to pour millions of dollars into the creation of think tanks mostly independent of universities. These institutions would conduct research supporting conservative causes and would publish books and reports, magazines and newspaper articles and lobby the media, as well as provide policy analyses and proposals for conservative politicians. These foundations have also endowed professorships in many universities in an attempt to increase conservative influence within them. Thus the Heritage Foundation and the American Enterprise Institute in Washington, D.C., and the Hoover Institution at Stanford University have been in direct service to Republican presidential administrations, members of Congress, and judges. From the 1980s to the present, the Republican-allied Olin, Scaife, and Bradley foundations have sponsored many books, magazines, and public television programs as platforms for conservative journalists and scholars on education and "the culture wars." Books sponsored by these organizations include Allan Bloom's *Closing of the American Mind,* Christina Hoff Sommers's *Who Stole Feminism?* and David Brock's *Real Anita Hill* and *The Seduction of Hillary Clinton* (portions of both had been published in *The American Spectator,* a flamboyantly conservative journal of opinion funded by billionaire Richard Mellon Scaife, who also funds the Scaife Foundation).[1] Several of the same sponsors and foundations fund conservative college student organizations such as Young America's Foundation, Intercollegiate Studies Institute, Young Americans for Freedom, and the Madison Center for Educational Affairs. Although many other think tanks and foundations have a liberal orientation, the only ones with a direct link to the Democratic Party are the Progressive Policy Institute, a branch of the centrist Democratic Leadership Council, with which Bill Clinton and Al Gore were affiliated, and more recently, the left-liberal Center for American Progress, which sponsors a Campus Progress organization.

Conservatives argue that their foundations and think tanks serve as a legitimate counterforce to more lavishly funded foundations like Ford, Rockefeller, Carnegie, and MacArthur, which support mainly liberal causes. Liberals argue that this is a **false analogy** on several points: unlike the conservative ones, these foundations are not exclusively involved with political issues, they do not have an overt political agenda or party affiliation, they do not act as agents of the corporations sponsoring them (indeed, some of the projects they fund are highly critical of such corporations), and they fund some conservative projects along with a majority of liberal ones whose nature makes them unlikely to receive corporate funding.

The rise of these conservative institutes has provoked a great deal of controversy, with liberals questioning the integrity of their research and charging them with conflict of interest and **special pleading**. Their defenders' rebuttal is that their overt partisanship serves legitimately to counterbalance the covert liberal partisanship of most university faculties (at least in the humanities and social sciences), journalists, and foundations. And the liberal counter-rebuttal is that liberal bias in these groups is a legitimate counterbalance to all the realms of American public discourse that are dominated by corporations—political lobbies, advertising and public relations, corporate-owned media, business-oriented academic departments, university trusteeships and administrations, and so on—and that most liberal scholars or journalists are not beholden to special interests funding them. Be that as it may, for our purposes here it is useful for you just to know that you are likely to get a liberal viewpoint in the courses and writing of university or research-institute scholars in the humanities or social sciences and that you should compare it with the viewpoint of professors in business-oriented courses and with information originating in conservative think tanks.[2]

The somewhat absurd nature of this politicization of research institutes was captured in a satirical column by Jon Carroll (*San Francisco Chronicle,* December 4, 1998, C20), "Thinking about Think Tanks":

> There are your right-wing think tanks and your left-wing think tanks. They are funded by people with agendas; they are stocked like trout streams with people of a particular ideological bent who produce papers that discover reasons why it Makes Sense to believe tweedle or, contrariwise, twaddle.
>
> The people in the think tanks are often described as "respected" or "distinguished." They are "scholars." They just sit and think and think, and when they are done thinking, they believe whatever the person who's paying them to think also believes.

Notes

1. In a 1997 article for *Esquire,* "Confessions of a Right-Wing Hit Man," and in his 2002 book *Blinded by the Right: The Conscience of an Ex-Conservative,* Brock tells of how he was dropped as a reporter by the *American Spectator* when that publication and Scaife found his book on Hillary Clinton insufficiently negative toward the Clintons. Scaife also withdrew his financial support from *American Spectator* when it did not pursue his personal campaign against President Clinton to his satisfaction.

2. Several books have been written on the history of these conservative think tanks, including Sidney Blumenthal, *The Rise of the Counter-Establishment: From Conservative Ideology to Political Power,* and Jean Stefancic and Richard Delgado, *No Mercy: How Conservative Think Tanks and Foundations Changed America's Social Agenda.* For personal accounts by former insiders in these circles who now criticize them for being **propaganda** organs of the Republican Party, see Michael Lind, *Up from Conservatism,* and David Brock, *Blinded by the Right* and *The Republican Noise Machine.*

Topics for Discussion and Writing

1. Write out the prestudy exercises individually, then in discussion groups compare notes on the extent to which the chapter modified your previous definitions.
2. As an individual or class research paper project, with the guidance of your teacher, survey empirical studies of the following forms of power in America (as well as in your state and local region). Among the following groups that exercise those forms, determine which support conservative, libertarian, liberal, or leftist causes, the Republican versus the Democratic Party, and which have and spend more money in each area. (Both lists are ordered randomly here to avoid implication of relative power.)

Forms of Power:

- Power of employers (to hire, fire, control wages and working conditions); power of employees (to organize, negotiate, strike, or resign)
- Representation in executive, legislative, judicial, and military branches of government
- Political party organizations
- Lobbies
- Political action committees and campaign contributions
- Control of media
- Public relations agencies and political consultants
- Foundations and research institutes (think tanks)
- Administration, teaching, and research in K–12, college, and university education

Groups Exercising Power:

- Labor unions
- K–12 and college administrators and teachers (considered separately)
- Large corporations, small businesses, and their collective organizations
- Wealthy individuals versus those in the middle class and poor
- Media owners and executives, advertisers, journalists, performers, and other employed personnel (consider each separately; see Chapter 3)
- Advocacy organizations: political, religious, civil rights, consumer, environmentalist, educational

3. Do a Google search for Glenn Beck's accusations against billionaire George Soros's liberal political and philanthropic activities, then compare them with Soros's article "My Philanthropy" in *New York Review of Books*. Do further research to find evidence in support of these two opposing views.
4. Regarding table 2.3, "Social Class and Political Attitudes, Left to Right," and the notes following it, discuss in groups or write about how closely this hypothesis matches your sense of these realities. Do some research on the sociology and economics of social class, or on social class and political affiliations, to test against this model.
5. Steve Brouwer's viewpoint in "If We Decided to Tax the Rich" (www.paradigmpublishers.com/books/BookDetail.aspx?productID=321369) is left-of-liberal, or radical left, to the extent that he is arguing for the benefits of European social democracy over American capitalism. On what points does he criticize the Democrats from the left? What different lines of argument might he make if he were advocating pure socialism or Communism rather than social democracy?
6. In an article titled "The Intellectual Class War," conservative polemicist David Horowitz refutes liberal and leftist claims that most Republicans and wealthy capitalists are opposed to the well-being of workers, the poor, minorities, and the environment. Read the article, in Horowitz's book *The Art of Political War*, and his ongoing support for his position on his website Discover the Networks, then compare his reasoning and evidence with those in Brouwer and other liberal or leftist polemicists.
7. "Most Americans are probably familiar with the notion that if leftist or even liberal values are pushed to extremes, they can lead toward Communism. Far fewer Americans understand that if conservative values are pushed to extremes, they can lead toward fascism." Debate the accuracy of these assertions, and for research do interviews with your friends and family members about their understanding of fascism.
8. Relate the subject and viewpoint of the cartoon at the beginning of Chapter 3 to the topics of these two chapters. Tom Tomorrow's cartoons appear in left-liberal journals like *Z Magazine* and *American Prospect*.

3
Thinking Critically about Mass Media

"This Modern World," by Tom Tomorrow

Do news, entertainment, and advertising media give the people what they want or control what people want? Can the media be objective, and *should* they be? How can it be that conservatives are convinced that the media have a left-wing bias while leftists are equally convinced the media have a right-wing bias? These issues are endlessly, heatedly debated by political partisans, media critics, and scholars. Once again, we must recognize the rhetorical and semantic ambiguities involved in addressing these questions in their full complexity. The present chapter develops some of the topics in Chapter 2 in specific reference to media, and the issues here parallel those about whether political elections and legislation truly represent the people, so it would be useful to review the concepts and definitions in that chapter. As in Chapter 2, this chapter attempts to arrive at definitions and judgments that are acceptable to leftists and rightists alike, while recognizing the extreme difficulty in doing so, and it is likewise open to refinement and revision at readers' suggestions.

DO THE MEDIA GIVE PEOPLE WHAT THEY WANT?

In a classic essay entitled "Masscult and Midcult" in his book *Against the American Grain,* Dwight Macdonald wrote,

> The masses are in historical time what a crowd is in space: a large quantity of people unable to express their human qualities because they are related to each other neither as individuals nor as members of a community. In fact, they are not related to *each other* at all.... Yet this collective monstrosity, "the masses," "the public" is taken as a human norm by the technicians of Masscult [mass culture]. They at once degrade the public by treating it as an object, to be handled with the lack of ceremony of medical students dissecting a corpse, and at the same time flatter it and pander to its taste and ideas by taking them as the criterion of reality....
>
>   Whenever a Lord of Masscult is reproached for the low quality of his products, he automatically ripostes, "But that's what the public wants, what can I do?" A simple and conclusive defense, at first glance. But a second look reveals that (1) to the extent the public "wants" it, the public has been conditioned to some extent by his products, and (2) his efforts have taken

this direction because (a) he himself also "wants" it—never underestimate the ignorance and vulgarity of publishers, movie producers, network executives and other architects of Masscult—and (b) the technology of producing mass "entertainment" (again, the quotes are advised) imposes a simplistic, repetitious pattern so that it is easier to say the public wants this than to say the truth which is that the public gets this and so wants it....

For some reason, objections to the giving-the-public-what-it-wants line are often attacked as undemocratic and snobbish. But it is precisely because I do believe in the potentialities of ordinary people that I criticize Masscult. (9–11)

Do—and *should*—mass news and entertainment media "give the people what they want"? Both sides of this question are equally complex. Do those running commercial media really know what the people want, in the sense that large numbers of people actively make known to media representatives what they would like to read, hear, and see? Or are the people mainly providing passive feedback to what they are offered, in the form of random surveys and ratings polls that are impersonal and imprecise at best? Macdonald suggests that there is a vicious circle or self-fulfilling prophecy here: the people are conditioned, to some extent, to want what they get, or at least to take what they get in the absence of any preferable alternatives. Have audiences asked for the constantly increasing number and length of commercials on TV and radio? Have pro sports fans asked for constantly longer seasons and multiplying numbers of teams and league divisions, or have they simply failed to resist the TV broadcasters' drive to increase coverage, and thus advertising revenue? Defenders of the media say no one is forced to watch or listen to anything, and everyone is free to take it or leave it. But critics like Macdonald ask, if we are all conditioned from the time we are infants to consume and accept media messages, are we really free to choose? (All these questions about the media parallel the questions about the whole, larger economic system of capitalism, of which the media form a key part, and the conservative assumption that consumers are free to take or leave the products the system produces. These questions are pursued further, in reference to public relations agencies, advertising, and hype in Chapters 4 and 5.)

Furthermore, if "the people" are considered to be the largest segment of the audience numerically, that means those at the literacy level of high school graduates or lower—and they are indeed defined by many media marketers as the target audience. This is the presumed audience for supermarket tabloids like the *National Enquirer,* for action movies filled with shoot-outs and explosions, for pro wrestling, talk radio shows, and TV and radio programs that parade outrageous sexual practices. Political **demagogues**, on the right or left, also give the people what they want, by appealing to the most uninformed and prejudiced segments of the population to win their support. This notion of "the people" as a mass of illiterates to be both pandered to and exploited by media and politicians, then, is quite removed from Thomas Jefferson's ideal of a nation of critical citizens whose education will have "raised the mass of the people to the high ground of moral respectability necessary to their own safety, and to orderly government" ("The Natural Aristocracy," 1308).

The argument can be made that, instead of appealing to the lowest common denominator in the public, at least some media should give the more informed and critical segment of the people what *it* wants. Certain media, which are not exclusively concerned with "bottom-line" profitability, do in fact appeal to that segment—such as journals of opinion, public broadcasting, C-SPAN, and influential national newspapers like the *New York Times* and *Wall Street Journal.* In other words, if the media were considered as a profession comparable to education, law, or medicine, wouldn't it be reasonable to expect its practitioners to be more knowledgeable about world and national events, culture, and the arts than the mass audience, and therefore to have a responsibility to inform, even to educate their audience, in the manner of teachers, rather than descending to the level of the lowest common denominator? (In this analogy, few people would say that teachers should gear their classes to the level of the least informed or most prejudiced students, or that doctors should just tell their patients what they want to hear, rather than expressing their informed medical judgments.) This responsibility to inform was in fact the original intention of the chartering of the public airwaves by the federal government in the 1920s, and the takeover of broadcasting (first radio, then television) by advertising was strongly opposed by large segments of public opinion, led by then Secretary of Commerce Herbert Hoover, who by the standards of that time was considered a conservative Republican. Hoover said that it was "inconceivable that we should allow so great a possibility for service ... to be drowned in advertising chatter," and that if a presidential message ever became "the meat in a sandwich of two patent medicine advertisements," it would destroy broadcasting (quoted in Eric Barnouw, *The Sponsor,* 15).

Traditionally, news divisions of national and local TV companies were not expected to garner high ratings or advertising revenue, and their losses were "carried" by owners out of some vestige of the public service concept at the origin of American broadcasting. This has changed in the past few decades, however, as news broadcasters have devised more profitable formats for what is now termed "infotainment," including "happy-talk" and "top-forty stories" featuring "If it bleeds, it leads" sensationalism. Other recent influences in the sensationalizing of newscasts include the proliferation of twenty-four-hour-a-day cable TV networks and the concentration of media ownership by megacorporations like Disney, Time-Warner, ABC-Capital Cities-Paramount, and Rupert Murdoch's News Corporation—which in 2007 added the *Wall Street Journal* to an empire including Fox TV and the *New York Post*. On this concentration, see Eric Alterman's 2003 book *What Liberal Media?* or download the more up-to-date video of Bill Moyers's PBS segment on December 7, 2012, "Big Media's Power Play," which begins, "In 1983, fifty corporations controlled a majority of American media. Now that number is six. And Big Media may get even bigger, thanks to the FCC's consideration of ending a rule preventing companies from owning a newspaper and radio and TV stations in the same city."

These megacorporations typically have imposed demands that newspapers and broadcast news meet a profit quota comparable to that of their more profitable divisions, with the result of drastic cutbacks in editorial staff, news coverage, in-depth reporting, commentary, and cultural pages. These cutbacks have been compounded by the shift of readership to the Internet, where online versions of news media do not have comparable advertising revenue and so cannot afford to maintain full editorial staffs. The same process has changed the book publishing industry, where corporate conglomerates have bought up relatively small, low-profit publishers and textbook companies, resulting in demands for higher profits. These demands in turn have led to "dumbing down" of content, increased prices, and more frequent new editions of the same textbooks to abort used-book resales. This trend has also been compounded by the monopolization of bookstores by big chains like Barnes and Noble and Borders, which in turn have been displaced by online giants like Amazon.

These, then, are some of the complexities and dangers of "giving the people what they want" mainly in terms of maximizing audiences, and these are some implicit arguments in favor of media producers instead exercising their own professional judgment and tastes in setting the media agenda. This alternative, however, can lead to the danger at the **equal and opposite extreme**—of the producers manipulating audiences into compliance with their own biases or special interests. As Dwight Macdonald put it in an earlier version of "Masscult and Midcult," comparing mass culture in capitalist and Communist countries, "The Lords of *kitsch* [a German term for mass culture], in short, exploit the cultural needs of the masses in order to make a profit and/or to maintain their class rule—in communist countries, only the second purpose prevails." So liberal and leftist critics play up instances of corporate owners and advertisers exploiting audiences to impose capitalist ideology, social conformity, trivial pursuits, and consumption of commodities as a "bread and circuses" distraction from critical political awareness, while conservatives play up instances of liberal media elites imposing their own self-interested politics in the manner Macdonald ascribes to Communists. Both sides here are apt to fall into the "heads I win, tails you lose" fallacy: when media bias favors their own side, they say the media are just giving the people what they want, but when bias favors the other side, they accuse the "media elite" of manipulating, and being contemptuous of, the people.

One final variable that needs to be factored in here (and that has received a lot of attention in recent media scholarship) is the extent to which audiences are capable of seeing through and resisting the ideological messages sent out by the media or of re-appropriating those messages to their own purposes, and how much they do so in daily practice. This is a trickier question than it may first appear. You might firmly believe that you are not "taken in" by advertising or political slanting in media, but can you be certain that you do not unconsciously absorb many culturally conditioned assumptions through the media? For example, Juliet Schor's book *The Overspent American* asserts that media images of upscale characters have prompted many Americans to go into debt to emulate their lifestyle: "Every additional hour of television a person watches each week increases that person's annual spending by about two hundred dollars." In contrast to earlier decades in which most Americans tried to keep up with the Joneses next door, these days, "they are more likely to judge themselves against the affluent yuppies who proliferate in shows" (90).

Topics for Discussion and Writing

1. Explain why you agree or disagree with Macdonald that the media do not treat audience members as individuals but as "masses."
2. Do you think that the media give you personally what you want? That you are completely free to "take it or leave it"? Or do you

think your wants may have been conditioned by the media? How can you know? Consider as test cases the influence of the media on your preferences in or attitudes toward one of the following: fashions in clothes and grooming; brand names; favorite TV programs, movies, magazines, websites, and social media; gender roles and identity, such as ideals of attractive women and men; spectator sports; popular music; news and politics; different ethnic groups and religions—e.g., Hispanics, Arabs, and Muslims; or performers or dramatic characters on TV and in other media as role models for lifestyle, as described by Juliet Schor above.
3. Macdonald says, "For some reason, objections to the giving-the-public-what-it-wants line are often attacked as undemocratic and snobbish." In other words, people tend to confuse criticisms like Macdonald's of the media for looking down on and manipulating the common people with criticisms of the people themselves. Try to explain Macdonald's distinction in your own terms, then explain why you agree or disagree with it.
4. In group discussions, see what examples various students come up with of people *not* being taken in by media manipulation but of having skeptical distance from media productions or turning them to their own personal, multicultural, or political purposes.
5. In connection with the discussion here of the dumbing down of news and other media under the influence of concentration of ownership and demands for increased profit margins, to what extent do you think these trends call into question (1) the operation of communication media for the purpose of corporate profit; (2) a broader fault in the ideology of "free enterprise" and the profit motive, in the tendency to aim at the lowest common denominator of taste or literacy in markets; and (3) the claims of conservatives to support moral principles in social issues while in economics they to tend to subordinate those principles to the defense of maximizing profits?
6. With regard to the quotation at the end of this section from Juliet Schor about the social classes depicted in sitcoms and other media, monitor several popular TV programs or current movies to research the extent to which "upper-middle-class, or even rich" people are still the norm.
7. The analogies were suggested above that at least some media should have an obligation to inform and educate the audience in the same way that teachers do, and that some media should resemble professions like medicine or law in expressing authoritative viewpoints rather than just catering to uninformed public opinion. Discuss and write about the extent to which you find these analogies valid.

ARE NEWS MEDIA OBJECTIVE? WHAT ARE THEIR BIASES?

The directors of news media often insist that they are committed to objectivity in their news pages or newscasts and that they limit subjective viewpoints to their editorial and opinion pages or broadcast commentaries. Scholars of the media, however, have pointed out dozens of subjective variables that color selection and presentation of the news in both print and broadcast media. A partial list of these factors includes ownership of media companies; hiring of editors and reporters, and assignment of stories to particular writers and editors; selection of what stories to cover and books to review, of sources interviewed and letters to the editor published, of prominence in space or time accorded different sources, and of headlines (written by editors, not writers); editing, sequencing, and abridging of writers' copy or camera footage; the institutional structure and conventions of news operations; and, of course, all of the rhetorical and semantic choices in every piece of writing or speaking that are discussed throughout this book.

Here is just one of an infinite number of possible illustrations of how journalists' subjective judgments, political and otherwise, come out in every day's news. During the 1998 senatorial election in New York, Rupert Murdoch's *New York Post,* which editorially endorsed the Republican incumbent Al D'Amato against the Democratic challenger Charles Schumer, at one point ran a front-page headline "Al Storms Ahead," followed by a story showing D'Amato leading in a poll by 1.3 percent. Shortly thereafter, a report that Schumer had gone ahead in the same poll by 4.2 percent was carried on an inside page with a smaller headline, "Chuck Squeaks Ahead of Al." Schumer won by 9 percent.

A conceivable alternative to our present conventions of print and broadcast news being presented in the form of a monologue, with no questioning of the reporter's or editor's bias, might be to present the news in a more self-reflexive, multi-perspectival format, in which several reporters and analysts with a variety of ideological viewpoints collaborate on the same story and take part in a dialogue on the problems presented by their own subjectivity on each issue. One program that successfully applied this approach was a former nightly feature on PBS station KQED-TV in San Francisco, *Newsroom of the Air.* In the current absence of widely available media like this, your best alternative as a critical consumer of the news is to gain regular access to the widest possible range of media and to learn to compare their viewpoints on a day-to-day basis.

> ## Topics for Discussion and Writing
>
> 1. Read a current newspaper or view a TV newscast or background report looking for ways in which reporters have injected their opinion into ostensibly neutral reports. Also look for examples of reports in which a successful effort has been made toward neutrality or balancing of opposed views.
> 2. As a group project with your classmates, prepare a mock broadcast on yesterday's news with a panel of students representing a conservative, liberal, libertarian, socialist, feminist, and ethnic viewpoint on the day's events.
> 3. In group discussions with classmates, brainstorm what alternative systems of communications (or means of diversifying our present one) might be feasible. For example, what about national and local print media or Internet equivalents to public broadcasting? Research existing alternative media in America and systems in other countries that differ significantly from ours. A good source here is *The Death and Life of American Journalism: The Media Revolution That Will Begin the World Again,* by Robert W. McChesney and John Nichols.

THE DEBATE OVER POLITICAL BIAS IN MEDIA

An attempt toward an evenhanded overview of this debate needs to be approached through further consideration of several of the complex rhetorical and semantic dimensions of the issue.

First Dimension: Ambiguity of Definitions

Once again, terms like *left, right, liberal, conservative, centrist, moderate, mainstream, middle of the road, radical,* and *extreme* have no fixed, universally agreed-on definitions but can only be accurately referred to in some specified context. Most people like to consider themselves moderate and mainstream, and few describe their views as radical or extremist. (An exception would be leftists who accept the designation of radical in the sense of the word related etymologically to "root" from the Latin *radix,* meaning that they believe in going to the root causes of social problems—e.g., the structure of capitalism—in contrast to what they perceive as the superficial policies of liberals who only deal with symptoms or effects while ignoring structural causes.) Often, "radical" and "extremist" are used merely as name-calling **dirties** against one's opponents; so if you want to use those labels legitimately, you need to provide concrete support for them.

Another ambiguity in *moderate, centrist,* and *middle of the road* is that, although such words usually carry a favorable connotation, positions described with these labels may sometimes just be vague, muddled, and noncommittal. It is possible for such positions to be adhered to (say, by news media or scholars) in a dogmatic manner that excludes a hearing for any positions outside a narrow range near the center—in which case, it is conceivable to speak of "the radical middle," "extremism of the center," or "immoderate moderation." Left-of-liberal Texas humorist Jim Hightower titled a book of his essays *There's Nothing in the Middle of the Road but Yellow Stripes and Dead Armadillos.*

Finally, we must always ask about "centrist" and "middle of the road" positions, what are they the center *of,* and what road are they the middle of? For example, in a worldwide perspective, both American politics and news media are to the right of the many democracies that have large socialist, Communist, and labor parties and presses. Some views that are considered radical left here are considered centrist in the social democracies of Western Europe, Canada, and Japan, while those called centrist would be considered rightist from those countries' perspectives. This is a very good reason to familiarize yourself, to the extent possible, with political views and media in countries that are not bound by American ethnocentrism.

A sarcastic commentary on this point was made in the *Los Angeles Times* by socialist journalist Alexander Cockburn after the election of Democrat Gray Davis as governor of California in 1998:

> "I am a moderate and a pragmatist by nature," Davis declared. "I will govern neither from the right nor the left, but from the center, propelled not by ideology but by common sense." This same common sense had prompted Davis earlier that day to meet with a platoon of lobbyists for the state's energy, agriculture and real estate sectors at which time the incoming governor assured them of his profound concern for their interests. If there were equivalent encounters that day with farm workers, nurses and

others from kindred walks of life, they escaped the attention of the press. As with Bill Clinton, centrism on Davis' terms means uncritical acceptance of the most abrasive of all ideologies: the belief that the role of government is to promote the corporate agenda. ("Gray Davis's Real Agenda: Corporatism," January 7, 1999, B9)

Another consequence of the skewing of the American balance to the right in a worldwide and historical context is that democratic socialists are sometimes labeled "radical leftists" in American politics and media, equated with "the radical right" of the Ku Klux Klan, American Nazis, racist or homophobic murderers, abortion-clinic bombers, violent militias, and right-wing death squads elsewhere in the world. Even many conservatives, however, would probably agree that this degree of extremism would characterize few current American socialists, although it might have applied in earlier decades to the Communist Party or violent groups that emerged briefly in the 1960s like revolutionary Marxist-Leninist sects. (This is not to imply that most conservative politicians or media figures, such as Rush Limbaugh and Glenn Beck, endorse right-wing extremism; the criticism they are open to is **selective vision** in downplaying denunciation of right-wing extremists while they disproportionately play up every fault they find in leftists.)

To reiterate yet another important semantic distinction from Chapter 2, debates between liberalism and conservatism concern both economic and social (or moral) issues, and media are not always consistent on their positions in these two realms. For example, corporate media like Disney or the Fox network, which generally support the conservative economic interests of their owners and advertisers, present some productions that are widely perceived as liberal in *moral* issues, like the many TV programs that now depict homosexuality positively, or the blasphemous obscenity of *South Park*—thereby convincing social conservatives of their liberal bias and providing leftists evidence of the hypocrisy of conservative business interests that preach traditional morality but practice whatever is profitable. Partisans of one side often **stack the deck** by playing up alleged bias in their opponents in media on the basis of the opponents' position on, say, moral issues like these while playing down their conflicting position on economic issues.

In their book *Watching America: What Television Tells Us about Our Lives,* S. Robert Lichter, Linda S. Lichter, and Stanley Rothman, whose research was funded by the conservative American Enterprise

Institute and Olin and Scaife foundations, nevertheless admirably avoid this kind of selective vision by presenting clearly qualified distinctions between the economic and moral realms, and between liberals and radical leftists, in summarizing the findings of their research on the backgrounds and attitudes of the creators of television entertainment. About those creators' "alienation" from mainstream American opinion, the authors say, "These findings suggest that the Hollywood community's political alienation is rooted in social rather than economic issues. In fact, it is their social liberalism that most clearly distinguishes them from the general public" (16). And, "Television preaches a kind of Porsche populism that reflects Hollywood's socially liberal and cosmopolitan sensibility.... This is not to say that TV entertainment has followed this agenda unreservedly or has engaged in anything like a radical critique of American society" (290).

Topics for Discussion and Writing

1. Find Link TV, the *Guardian*, BBC News, or Al Jazeera on cable TV or the Internet and compare their reports on a day's news with coverage on the American networks. Livestation.com provides links to these and a variety of other international English-language news sources.
2. Read several left-of-liberal journals of opinion like *The Nation, In These Times, Mother Jones*, the *Progressive, Z Magazine,* and *Extra!* to see if their viewpoint strikes you as "radical" or "extreme." Do they distance themselves from forms of left-wing extremism such as Communism? Read some conservative journals of opinion like *American Spectator*, the *Weekly Standard*, and *National Review*, or listen to Rush Limbaugh, Ann Coulter, and Glenn Beck to see if they are as critical of right-wing radicals as they are of leftist ones or even mainstream liberals. That is, do they identify themselves as mainstream conservatives or extreme rightists? Do they acknowledge the existence of right-wing extremism and distance themselves from it?
3. In an individual or group research project, monitor TV news and magazines, dramatic and entertainment shows, or current films to see if you find a distinction between liberal or conservative viewpoints on social (or moral) issues—for example, religion, abortion, drugs, feminism, sexual promiscuity, obscenity, homosexuality—versus economic ones such as depictions of different socioeconomic classes (the rich, the poor, and the middle class; professionals versus blue-collar workers; employers versus employees).

4. In the quoted column by Alexander Cockburn, explain his use of irony in the phrase "this same common sense" and his between-the-lines refutation of Governor Davis's claim that he is "propelled not by ideology."
5. Lichter, Lichter, and Rothman coined the phrase "Porsche populism." This is a figure of speech called an *oxymoron,* a form of paradox in which two words generally considered opposites are linked. What is your understanding of what they mean by this phrase?

Second Dimension: Relativity of Viewpoint

For an explanation of why conservatives see only left-wing bias in the media and leftists see only right-wing bias, let's come back to the spectrum of American media and commentators from left to right in Chapter 2 (table 2.2). In the table, the division of sections A and B into four columns is an arbitrary semantic oversimplification of what could be broken down into several more columns or even a continuous, linear spectrum from left to right. Many of these placements are also disputable, to be sure, and subject to revision as different media and individuals periodically shift their positions.

If your viewpoint is that of the far right, you are obviously going to consider all the other points on the spectrum biased toward the left, while if your viewpoint is far left, you will consider all the others biased toward the right. This is not to say that the views from either end of the spectrum are inaccurate or eccentric. In section A, the media in columns 1 and 4 are more overtly partisan than those in columns 2 and 3. Most of those in column 4 overtly support conservatism and the Republican Party (although they disagree among themselves over the degree and nature of conservatism the Republicans should stand for; see the discussion of differences among conservatives in Chapter 2). Most in column 1 in both sections A and B are to the left of the mainstream of the Democratic Party and of the media in A-2 and A-3, and of the individuals in B-2. Whether overtly socialistic or not, they are more critical than liberals of the Democratic Party, capitalism, and nationalism; more strongly pro-labor, multicultural, and feminist; and inclined to support leftist third parties, such as (most recently) the New Party, the Labor Party, and the Green Party. Fairness and Accuracy in Reporting (FAIR), Media Matters, *The Nation,* Edward Herman, and Noam Chomsky criticize the true conservatism of the "liberal" media more than they do the overtly conservative media; when the "liberal" media acknowledge such criticisms at all, it is usually to dismiss the "radical" left with contempt.

By contrast to columns 1 and 4 in section A and columns 1 and 3 in section B, the media in section A-2 and A-3, and the individuals in section B, column 2, are not overtly affiliated with one political party or ideology, and they insist on their commitment to neutrality or objectivity. In practice, however, many in section A-2, column 2, and section B-2, lean toward the liberal wing of the Democratic Party and its policies, although their support of Democrats, capitalism, and American nationalism clearly positions them to the right of those in column 1. Some in section A-3, however, and in section B-2, tend toward the more conservative wing of the Democratic Party (Clinton-Gore-Kerry) and the more liberal wing of the Republican Party. So when Republicans make the case that the media in section A-3 have a liberal or left bias, they could perhaps more accurately argue that the bias is liberal-centrist, to the left of conservative Republicans but to the right of those in columns 1 and 2.

Moreover, the media in table section A-2, and even more so in section A-3, attempt to maintain a degree of balance between liberal and conservative views, especially in their commentators and columnists; the *New York Times* op-ed page, for example, currently has regular columns by liberals Paul Krugman, Gail Collins, Charles Blow, Nicholas Kristof, and Maureen Dowd, conservatives David Brooks, Ross Douthat, and Thomas Friedman (a liberal on most issues but conservative as an influential advocate of globalization, as in his book *The World Is Flat*). Sections A-2 and A-3 are only occasionally open to either libertarian or left-of-liberal views. The *Los Angeles Times*'s former "Column Left/Column Right" was one of the few major op-ed sections in the country that regularly featured leftists like Alexander Cockburn, Robert Scheer, and feminist Ruth Rosen—all of whom lost their positions when the paper was taken over by more conservative, bottom-line-oriented owners. Few of the conservative media in A-4 grant any regular time or space at all to liberal or left authors, though they do sometimes include libertarians. These refinements indicate that there may be good reason for those on the far right to consider all the media to the left of them to be biased against their clearly articulated conservative position, and for those on the far left to feel the same way about all the other positions opposed to their own clear-cut position. (All of which is to reiterate the value of having regular exposure to sources on the far left and far right, to gain understanding of their clear-cut viewpoints in contrast to the frequent muddle of opinions in the mainstream media.) Those on the far left and far right do, however, tend to ignore all the degrees of difference among and within the positions other than far left or far right. (Another axiom of rhetorical ethnocentrism is that we are all inclined to play up significant differences among those we are most familiar with, but to downplay differences among our opponents and to consider them a monolithic bloc.)

Since its founding in 1996 by Rupert Murdoch, the international media mogul, Fox News has broken new ground as an overtly partisan network in the style of print journals of opinion. Its slogan "Fair and Balanced" refers to its news coverage rather than its opinion shows, though it is perhaps a tongue-in-cheek comment on Fox's mission to counteract the alleged liberal bias of "the mainstream media," including CNN, which defines itself as middle-of-the-road. However, at least until recently, few mainstream media have professed openly to favor liberalism or the Democratic Party, nor have their executives and primary journalists generally been directly connected to the Democratic Party. By contrast, Murdoch is an outspoken Republican supporter and Fox's president Roger Ailes was previously a Republican presidential media consultant, while its commentators and talk-show lineups, whose regulars have included Sarah Palin, Mike Huckabee, and Karl Rove, constitute a Republican "Who's Who." The documentary DVD *Outfoxed: Rupert Murdoch's War on Journalism* makes a case that even Fox's news reports are controlled to push a Republican line.

Since about the 2006 elections, as liberalism in general has seen a revival, outspoken liberals have become more prominent in the media, such as Arianna Huffington on Huffington Post and frequent TV appearances, Jon Stewart and Stephen Colbert on Comedy Central, and Bill Maher on HBO. Most significantly, MSNBC and Current TV have positioned themselves to the left of CNN. The popularity of Bill O'Reilly and other conservatives on Fox News has been rivaled by MSNBC's and Current TV's lineups of outspokenly Democratic commentators (most prominently Keith Olbermann, first on MSNBC, then on Current TV, though more recently on neither). Current TV was started by former Democratic vice president Al Gore, and, among MSNBC's talk show hosts, Al Sharpton was once a Democratic presidential candidate, while Chris Matthews and Lawrence O'Donnell have worked for Democratic officeholders.

> ## *Topics for Discussion and Writing*
>
> 1. As a collective exercise, conduct a survey within your class based on table 2.2 in Chapter 2. Have every student add up the number of people in each of the four columns whom (1) they have heard of, and (2) they remember seeing on TV, hearing on radio, or reading in newspapers, magazines, and the Internet. Collate the results and see if any inferences are warranted about which points on the spectrum are most favored by the media.
> 2. Discuss in class how valid everyone finds the placement of media figures in the four columns of table 2.2 as well as the breakdown of the columns themselves. Suggest alternatives, perhaps for more columns providing for finer distinctions among positions on the left or right.
> 3. Watch *Outfoxed* on DVD to evaluate how persuasively it supports the argument that Fox News's claim to be "Fair and Balanced" is untrue. Is *Outfoxed* itself fair and balanced?

Third Dimension: Diverse Influences in Media

Every day, media "watchdog" organizations on the right like the Media Research Center (mrc.org) and FrontPage Magazine (frontpagemag.com) "cherry pick" every example of liberal bias, and those on the left like Media Matters (mediamatters.org) and FAIR (fair.org) do the opposite. When we read the conservative views, the evidence they present of liberal bias in media seems overwhelming; yet when we read articles by leftists on the same topic, their evidence for conservative bias seems equally persuasive. What, then, can we conclude from a comparative reading of the opposing sides? Perhaps that each side is using selective vision, stacking the deck by playing up every cause and instance of bias on the other side while downplaying every one of bias on its own? (This is a classic case of the "Predictable Patterns of Political Rhetoric" in Chapter 2.) Thus the most plausible answer to the question of whether the media have a liberal or a conservative bias is "both"—the bias is sometimes and in some ways liberal (though almost never explicitly socialistic) and at other times and in other ways conservative. This is not necessarily to imply that there is a 50-50 balance, only that we need to take an evenhanded overview of partisan viewpoints supporting the opposing camps, carefully weigh the evidence presented by opposing sources, and recognize more complexities in the issue than acknowledged by partisans on either side, in order to arrive at our own judgment of what the actual balance might be.

As anyone who has worked in commercial media (including me) will attest, "the media" aren't a monolithic entity but are organizations in which several opposing forces are jockeying for dominance every day. These forces include at least the following, in no fixed order of influence:

- Employees: editors and writers in print media; producers, directors, newscasters, and performers in television, films, radio, concerts, and recordings
- Owners and executives of media corporations ("management" as opposed to employees or "labor")
- Advertisers
- Pressure groups, public relations agencies, and lobbyists, including those of corporations, government, political parties, public-policy foundations and research institutes, and consumer advocates
- Audiences

Among these groups, at both the national and local levels, most individual or corporate owners of media corporations, their appointed top executives, and major advertisers are in the wealthiest stratum, and thus by definition most can be expected to be conservative, in the sense of supporting capitalism and a corporate social order. Their party affiliation has more often been Republican than Democratic, with exceptions like many "Hollywood liberal" movie executives and Ted Turner, who founded CNN, although neither Turner nor most Hollywood liberals are opponents of capitalism; CNN is now owned by the more conservative Time-Warner. Another partial exception would be newspapers like the *New York Times, Washington Post,* and *Los Angeles Times* (when it was owned by the Chandler family), which are owned by families with long-established wealth and dedication to public service, and who thus are willing to subordinate direct editorial control and maximizing of profit to maintain their papers' reputations for the independence of their journalist employees. But here again, leftists argue that these media are still ultimately organs of corporate capitalism, albeit self-styled "responsible capitalism."

Most public relations agencies, lobbies, foundations, and research institutes that represent big business are conservative, while those that represent labor unions and citizen-advocacy groups like Common

Cause, People for the American Way, and the Sierra Club are liberal. Various segments of government also employ public relations agents and researchers, and their politics will vary according to whether the particular agency employing them tends to be conservative (such as the Defense Department—see Chapter 4) or liberal (such as the Environmental Protection Agency), and according to the ideology of the party currently in office. As for audiences, they obviously contain the same proportion of liberals and conservatives that the electorate does at any particular time. To the extent that the media attempt to "give the people what they want," some media try to target either the liberal or the conservative audience, while others try to work both sides of the street, with vague or mixed political messages.

The politics of the various kinds of media employees in section B-2 of table 2.2 is more complicated. Media scholars generally agree that this group includes the most liberals, at least relatively, in comparison to groups 3 and 4. Those select media employees who become "stars" are sometimes an exception to the rule equating wealth with conservatism, their politics often being that of the Hollywood Democrat, limousine liberal, or Porsche populist variety, retaining the affiliation of most artists and intellectuals with the Democratic Party—see Chapter 2, table 2.3, "Social Class and Political Attitudes." Nevertheless, when those in this group become multimillionaires as performers, news anchors, analysts, or talk show hosts—as many have in recent decades—and when they become social peers and associates of political leaders and wealthy executives, many experience the conservatizing force of wealth, status, and power. Leftist journalist David Sirota, writing for *In These Times,* criticizes such media journalists whose high income distorts their view of economic issues, as when MSNBC's self-identified liberal Chris Matthews said, "Am I part of the winner's circle in American life? I don't think so." Sirota points out that Matthews's annual salary is $5 million, he has three Mercedes, and lives in Chevy Chase, Maryland, a favored suburb of the Washington establishment. In any case, few media liberals come close to the $38 million a year that staunch conservative Rush Limbaugh is currently paid. (Comparing liberal and conservative media figures' wealth would be a good research project.)

All of the above forces try to impose their own viewpoint in the daily workings of the media. None of these forces prevail all the time or without conflict and accommodation. (Sometimes the conflicting forces result in self-contradiction or **compartmentalization**, as when the *New York Times*'s and the *New Yorker*'s liberal editorial content, sympathizing with the poor and opposing a growing wealth gap, is juxtaposed with advertisements for $10,000 Cartier jewelry, $700 Gucci shoes, and multimillion-dollar homes aimed at a limousine-liberal audience.) Liberals argue that owners have ultimate control over media content through the power of the pocketbook, including the power to hire and fire employees, but conservatives point to many examples in which the employees' views prevail over the owners'. Liberals also argue that owners and advertisers attempt to control content in a manner calculated to maximize profits and create a pro-corporate and nationalistic agenda, while conservatives respond that if a leftist media production, writer, or performer, is popular enough, and if the liberal or left-of-liberal audience is large or affluent enough, owners and advertisers at least sometimes will subordinate their ideological preferences to the propagation of an opposing but more profitable message. So conservatives point to Michael Moore's films as evidence that leftists can become wealthy through appealing to a progressive/populist audience, and they consider him a hypocrite for attacking corporations and the wealthy while enriching himself by doing so. Moore's *Fahrenheit 9/11* was dropped for distribution by Disney, allegedly under political pressure, but was picked up by Miramax and became very profitable. Leftists point to other instances where corporate ideology trumps popularity, such as that of Moore's *TV Nation,* a documentary series satirically criticizing corporations, which had high ratings on Fox but was canceled by right-wing billionaire Rupert Murdoch when he bought that network, or Jim Hightower's talk radio show, which was dropped by ABC when it bought up the network that was carrying it. So leftists see a vicious circle, in which prior restraint on leftist views precludes the theoretical possibility of their gaining a profitable audience.

Noncommercial public television and radio in America through most of the last half of the twentieth century presented many more leftist views than did commercial broadcasting, from which it can plausibly be inferred that commercial ownership and advertising do indeed tend to impose conservative economic views, and that funding by government and other noncorporate sources (e.g., audience contributors, colleges) does not necessarily lead to government control or censorship of content, which conservatives use as an **appeal to fear** against public broadcasting. (*Bill Moyers' Journal* on PBS was probably the most liberal program on TV, and also the most intellectual. A Republican chair of the Corporation for Public Broadcasting, Kenneth Tomlinson, pressured PBS to cancel Moyers's show, but after Tomlinson himself was forced to resign for excessive interference in what is chartered as an independent agency, it was brought back. So in this case, the attempt at government control was a conservative one.) Likewise for C-SPAN, which is noncommercial though funded as a public service by commercial broadcasters, and which presents congressional hearings, political speeches, extensive panels on public affairs, academic conferences, and book discussions, with a balance of liberal and conservative sources. Most other democracies today have much more publicly funded broadcasting and some print media, and likewise tend to be more liberal than American commercial media. In the past few decades, however, American conservative politicians have tried to eliminate or drastically reduce government funding for public television and radio (in a 2012 presidential debate, Mitt Romney joked that he would defund Big Bird and moderator Jim Lehrer of PBS) and to replace government support with corporate "underwriting" (often a euphemism for direct sponsorship and control of content in production), with the direct result of an increase in conservative views—for example, *Suze Orman: The Courage to Be Rich*.

Topics for Discussion and Writing

1. An extraordinary *60 Minutes* segment, "Confessions of a Tobacco Lobbyist" (March 19, 1995), clearly had a liberal viewpoint critical of the big business of tobacco and corporate lobbying of government officials. Although tobacco advertising is now banned on TV, the major tobacco companies form part of larger conglomerates, such as RJR-Nabisco, that are large TV advertisers and are quite possibly represented on the networks' boards of directors (you might research this). To what extent, then, did this report provide evidence for the conservative argument that media content is controlled by liberal producers rather than advertisers or corporate management? In your memory of TV news reports and magazine shows like *60 Minutes,* would you judge that such strong criticism of the tobacco industry, big business in general, and its lobbying of politicians is the rule or the exception? Research stories about efforts by the tobacco industry to suppress negative media reports about it, including another *60 Minutes* report on a cover-up by the tobacco industry of the addictive effects of nicotine. The popular Hollywood film *The Insider* was a thinly fictionalized account of this broadcast; study that film to analyze its viewpoint and possible bias.
2. Monitor print and broadcast coverage of strikes, protests against globalization of the economy and sweatshop labor, and other labor-management conflicts to see whether the coverage sympathizes

with one side or the other. Look for positive or negative images of business executives and labor unions projected in both news and entertainment media. How much do you think ownership of media by unions rather than corporations would alter such coverage?
3. Monitor programming on PBS television or NPR radio for a week and compare it to programming on the commercial networks and local stations. What differences and similarities do you find, and what is their ideological significance? Note who "underwrote" programs and whether the underwriter's influence is obvious. Discuss the positive and negative effects of the decline in public funding and increasing influence of corporate underwriters, and the question of how public broadcasting *should* differ from commercial media. Also compare C-SPAN, which has no corporate funding other than fees from the cable companies that carry it, or Pacifica Radio and its web streaming, funded mainly through subscriptions and private donations.

Fourth Dimension: Political Viewpoints and Levels of Education

A comparison of columns 1 and 4 in both sections A and B of table 2.2 in Chapter 2 reveals a peculiarity of American media. Many of the media and personalities in column 4 are among the most widely circulated in the country—for example, Fox News, *Reader's Digest,* Rush Limbaugh, and Glenn Beck, along with most regional newspapers, TV, and radio, which serve for the most part as boosters of local business interests and have less of a "wall" between editorial and ownership and advertising divisions than the national media. However, none of the media in section A-1 of table 2.2 and few of the personalities in B-1 have circulation anywhere comparable to those in A and B, column 4. One reason for the large circulation of many of the media and individuals in column 4 (and of most other mass-circulation print and broadcast media) is that their rhetoric is aimed at the widest possible audience—that is, the majority of the public, with an average literacy level of a high school graduate or less. At the other end of the spectrum, all of the left-of-liberal media and most of the individuals in column 1 of sections A and B address a more limited audience, mainly at a college-graduate level; their editors and writers tend to have strong academic credentials in liberal education (many hold PhDs) and are clearly identifiable as intellectuals.

A major historical irony here is that the politics of the left in the past centuries was that of the proletarian masses and the politics of conservatism was that of upper-class elites, but over the course of the twentieth century, at least in the United States, the masses moved toward the right and tended to align with the wealthy, so that conservative interests have preempted the image of populism, while the American left has shrunk to a constituency largely characterized by intellectuals (with exceptions including the remnants of militant labor unions, the poor, racial minorities, and immigrants), with the result that conservatives now stigmatize the left as the realm of "the cultural elite," entrenched in liberal arts departments of universities, small-circulation journals of opinion, public television and radio, and other intellectual media, and out of touch with the mainstream of American opinion. It is significant that PBS previously was the main TV and radio outlet for classical music, ballet, opera, and Broadway theater, but as it has been taken over by corporate underwriters and producers, it has added more "lowbrow" music—pop, country, and rock—along with local high school football championships, while NPR has added commentary on sports as well as pop music.

To be sure, some of the conservative media and individuals in column 4 are comparable to those in column 1 in their intellectual level. Journals of opinion like *Commentary,* the *Weekly Standard,* and *National Review,* as well as scholarly journals like *American Enterprise* and *Policy Review,* are edited and written by individuals, and are addressed to an audience at the same postcollegiate level. (To reiterate, that is why these journals make more credible conservative sources for college-level papers than mass-media conservatives like Rush Limbaugh.) So while there are intellectual media and spokespeople addressing an educated audience on the American right as well as the left, the *mass* media provide little voice for either the intellectual right or left, mainly because they limit expression to "sound bites" and oversimplifications, excluding the kind of extended, complex discourse that characterizes university-level courses and writing. This contrast is clear in the exceptions like C-SPAN, which regularly broadcasts university and research-institute conferences from both left and conservative sources.

Although the mass media tend to exclude intellectuals on both the right and the far left, leftists argue that the positions of the intellectual right do not differ as much from mainstream conservatism as those of the intellectual far left do from mainstream liberalism (intellectual leftists generally being more critical of the Democratic Party, in favor of socialist alternatives, than intellectual rightists are of the Republicans). As a result, the far left is the one position on the American political spectrum with least access to mass media (other than the extreme right of neo-Nazis, white supremacists, and militias, which has few intellectually reputable representatives). The more fair-minded conservatives acknowledge this fact, though they tend to downplay the difference between leftists and liberals, or else they speculate that in recent decades, ideas from the intellectual left have "trickled down" little by little into mainstream media, as Lichter, Lichter, and Rothman argue in *Watching America*:

> Television thus stands at the end of a long chain of popularization that begins with the creation of ideas and issues in universities, think tanks, "public interest" groups, and the like. The process continues with their entry into what Herbert Gans calls "upper middle" popular culture via the prestige press and "quality" magazines like *Atlantic* and *The New Yorker*. The most simplified version reaches the mass public in TV movies, "realist" dramatic series, and socially conscious sitcoms. (297)

Be that as it may, the practical implication of this analysis is that to get a full range of informed opinions, you should familiarize yourself with the ideas of intellectual leftists on university faculties and in books and journals of opinion, because you are unlikely to see or hear much of their ideas *firsthand,* without their being watered down through the "chain of popularization," in mass media.

Leftists argue that another reason their viewpoints do not receive an equal hearing in mass media is that most conservative ideas—such as patriotism, orthodox religion, family values, free enterprise, low taxes, commodity consumption, and strong support of the military, police, the right to bear arms, and "getting tough on criminals"—are not only more easily simplified and instinctively appealing to the mass audience but also are more congenial to wealthy media owners and advertisers with an interest in maximizing their profits and maintaining the status quo of consumer society. Leftists have long argued that "mass culture" in general has a conservative bias because it appeals to the lowest common denominator of cognitive development and to "conservative" blocks to critical thinking—nationalistic ethnocentrism, authoritarianism and conformity, ethnic prejudice and stereotyping, rationalization of the status quo, and so on. (For a comprehensive survey of this line of argument, see *American Media and Mass Culture: Left Perspectives,* Donald Lazere, ed.)

Another significant difference between left and right intellectual journals of opinion, which you can easily verify for yourself, is that most on the right have far more corporate advertisers and funding (billionaires Rupert Murdoch and Richard Mellon Scaife funded the *Weekly Standard* and *American Spectator,* respectively, while the Olin, Scaife, and Bradley foundations have funded others), and are more slickly produced, while most left journals barely survive on low advertising and sales, supplemented by donations from subscribers and occasional wealthy "angels" (liberal billionaire George Soros recently being one of the most prominent) acting out of conscience against their own class interests in supporting journals critical of the wealthy. So leftists argue that corporate ownership and advertising create conflicts of interest for the conservative intellectual journals.

A few of the individuals in section B-1, such as Michael Moore, Ralph Nader, the late Molly Ivins, Jim Hightower, Will Durst, and Paula Poundstone, do attempt to attain a populist appeal in their style and intended audience. Columns by Democratic Socialists of America members Barbara Ehrenreich and Harold Meyerson sometimes appear in *Time* and the *Washington Post,* but few of the more intellectual left commentators are allowed on the major TV discussion shows other than MSNBC or have prominent roles in the Democratic Party (from which Nader separated himself as an independent candidate for president), and none have reached the mass audience of Limbaugh, Pat Robertson, or Pat Buchanan (both Robertson and Buchanan have run for the Republican presidential nomination).

MSNBC's "talking heads" have, significantly, included several from left intellectual journals, along with Rachel Maddow, a PhD in political science, and Michael Eric Dyson, a professor of sociology and black studies. By the 2010s, MSNBC featured two Sunday morning talk shows, two hours each, hosted by Chris Hayes, a *Nation* editor and English professor, and Melissa Harris-Perry, a political science professor and *Nation* columnist. Their guests were also mainly scholars, intellectual journalists, and social activists—most liberal or leftist, but in civil, extended dialogue with conservative counterparts. At this writing, these programs appear to have attracted both sizeable audiences and corporate sponsorship, leading to an incongruous clash between the intellectual tone of the programs and their constant interruption by inane commercials. It remains to be seen how long and how far the sponsors will allow those on these programs to go on biting the corporate hand that feeds them or extending discussions beyond sound-bite length—and how long those on them will put up with the embarrassments of commercial sponsorship.

Another medium in which leftists have recently been dominant is documentary film. Following the success of Michael Moore, independent producers like Brave New Films and the Media Education Foundation have made political documentaries filmed and marketed at low cost, mainly through DVD sales and rentals; two prominent ones have been Robert Greenwald's *Outfoxed: Rupert Murdoch's War on Journalism* and *The Corporation*, a Canadian production distributed by Zeitgeist Films.

> ## *Topic for Discussion and Writing*
>
> What alternatives can you and classmates envision that would make the media more open to those who have informed opinions without representing wealthy interests? (C-SPAN would be one model here, in its presentations by scholars and authors of in-depth journalistic books.) What about a national TV channel or web journal that would be a version of a liberal arts college as a forum for the study of public controversies by faculty and students? Good topics for a research paper are various alternatives to "the mainstream media" including the "blogosphere"; Internet-based, nonprofit political and media organizations; and alternative media movements (e.g., FreePress.net, Pacifica Radio).

ASSIGNMENT FOR A PAPER

Write a thousand-word review (three or four typewritten pages) of a recent issue of a left-wing journal of opinion and a right-wing one. Get these from the periodical room at your campus or public library, from the Internet, or from a newsstand or bookstore. Recommended right-wing journals: *Weekly Standard, National Review, American Spectator, Washington Times Weekly, Human Events, Reason* (libertarian); left-wing ones: *The Nation, In These Times*, the *Progressive, Z Magazine, Extra!, Mother Jones.*

Read through all the articles, ads, and cartoons in both journals and, in about half the paper, summarize the scope of articles (and ads) in both, indicating to what extent the general range of topics and viewpoints reflects the left or right positions and patterns of rhetoric in Chapter 2, "Thinking Critically about Political Rhetoric." (Remark on any notable exceptions.) Then focus on one article in each that you find interesting and that expresses a left or right position particularly clearly or effectively, and summarize how it does so in as much detail as space allows. Also try to figure out whether the leftist magazine in general, and in your specific article, is liberal or socialist/left-of-liberal (i.e., does it criticize the Democrats from the left?), and whether the one on the right is mainstream Republican Party conservative or libertarian conservative (i.e., does it criticize the Republicans on libertarian terms?).

It might make it more interesting for you if you can find articles in the two journals on the same subject, so that you can note the opposing lines of argument. This is not essential, though, and do not try to get into a point-by-point comparison of the opposing lines, since this would make the paper too long.

The purpose of this assignment is to give you practice in understanding how the general rhetorical patterns of opposition between the left and right come out on particular current issues. Therefore, limit yourself to identifying these patterns objectively, *without expressing your opinions about the quality of the magazine or about particular articles and their arguments.* Do comment briefly, however, on whether either journal gave you a clearer understanding of the viewpoint it expresses than you had before, and in what way.

4

Special Interests and Propaganda

SPECIAL INTERESTS, CONFLICT OF INTEREST, AND SPECIAL PLEADING

The significance of the terms *special interests, conflict of interest,* and *special pleading* in argumentative rhetoric hinges on definitions of both the words *interest* and *special* that differ from everyday usage. When we say that someone is "an interested party" in a dispute, that "it is in her interest to support this policy," or that "his argument is self-interested," we do not mean that the person simply is interested in the subject; "to have an interest" here refers to having an investment or stake (financial or otherwise) in the outcome, some personal benefit. The term *disinterested,* as in "disinterested research," refers approvingly to the neutral, objective rhetorical stance of a speaker or writer who has no personal stake in an issue. (Note that *disinterested* is not synonymous with *uninterested,* though it is often misused that way.)

Likewise, *special* here is synonymous with a private, often selfish motive for support of a public policy. *Merriam-Webster's Collegiate Dictionary* defines *special interest* as "a person or group having an interest [as in *investment*] in a particular part of the economy and receiving or seeking special advantages therein often to the detriment of the general public." **Special pleading**, then, refers to people arguing for a position that they present as being in the public's benefit when it is secretly for the benefit of special interests. So special pleading typically uses the one-sided tactics of **propaganda** and **stacking the deck** to conceal the fact that the speaker or writer is presenting only the side of an issue that favors the interests being served. Most advertising, public relations, and lobbying messages are obvious forms of special pleading.

Conflict of interest is a financial investment or some kind of affiliation that is likely to bias the views of a speaker or writer. (Note that this concept differs from the simple term *conflict* in the sense of a disagreement, so be careful not to confuse them in your usage.) The classic conflict of interest situation is that of a government official who either stands to benefit personally from particular legislation or who has taken money from someone who does, such as a campaign contributor or lobbyist. In a famous episode of the 1950s, President Dwight Eisenhower's nominee for secretary of defense was the president of General Motors, Charles Wilson, whose confirmation was challenged because of conflicts of interest concerning GM's profits as a major military contractor. He testified that there was no conflict because "What's good for General Motors is good for America."

Conflict of interest becomes a rhetorical issue when it leads to special pleading, as when a legislator who has a personal financial investment benefited by pending legislation conceals that fact and makes a speech falsely arguing that the legislation is in the public interest. When you use statements by public officials as sources, you should try to find out what conflicts of interest might be biasing the views presented.

Other sources of information that you may draw on in researching papers are also subject to conflicts of interest. Journalistic sources may have conflicts involving owners', advertisers', or reporters' financial investments in issues reported on. The findings of journalists' or scholars' research might benefit or be harmful to special interests affiliated with the foundation or research institute subsidizing the research, in which case there might be explicit or tacit pressure on the researcher that taints the findings. Professors sometimes have investments in, or are paid consultants for, businesses or political interests that their research benefits—a situation that may also taint their teaching or published findings and conflict with university faculties' code of ethical disinterestedness. In one such case, according to the *Chronicle of Higher Education,* "Tobacco companies financed the work of several university scientists who published research and offered testimony that minimized the dangers of smoking" (http://chronicle.com, December 19, 1997). (Also see Mildred K. Cho, "Secrecy and Financial Conflicts of Interest in University-Industry Research Must Get Closer Scrutiny," *Chronicle of Higher Education,* August 1, 1997.) Teachers in public schools and universities have an obvious conflict of interest when they teach the pros and cons of increased taxes and spending for education, and if they belong to a teachers' union, they have a similar conflict in teaching about labor issues. In recent decades, conservatives have defined teachers, media employees, and other professionals and intellectuals as members of a "new class" that allegedly advocate liberal policies primarily because they serve the selfish interests of that class. [*Reader advisory: In the interests of full disclosure, I have been an employee of a public university and member of a teachers' union.*]

There are several other forms of conflict of interest beyond financial ones. Nepotism (favor toward relatives) and cronyism (favor toward friends) are also possible sources of conflicts of interest in many areas of public life. Journalistic reviews of books, films, recordings and concerts, restaurants, and other cultural topics are susceptible to distinctive kinds of conflict of interest. Advertising in a journal is often a trade-off for a review of the product, especially a positive one. When the same corporation owns the medium in which the review appears as well as the book publisher or film or recording company producing the work reviewed, there may be pressure from management for a favorable review. Journalist John Podhoretz, writing in the *Weekly Standard* (December 8, 1997), used impudent humor to deal with such a situation. After praising a film produced by Rupert Murdoch's Twentieth Century Fox, he made this "obligatory disclosure: Twentieth Century Fox is owned by News Corporation, which owns the *Weekly Standard* as well as the *New York Post,* my current employer. Now drop dead" (39).

Reviewers of books are subject to a variety of possible conflicts of interest, and the choice of assignments to freelance reviewers presents a constant test of the fair-mindedness of the editors of supplements such as the Sunday *New York Times Book Review,* in terms of conflicts of interest as well as ideological bias and avoiding assignments to either friends or enemies of the author. Editors' own biases can be discerned if they consistently solicit reviewers who they know in advance will be either favorably or unfavorably disposed toward a certain book. When I was chosen to review an anthology of articles for one such Sunday supplement, the editor would not allow me to say anything about one article because it quoted approvingly from a book of mine. Under a different editor, though, the same supplement later allowed a writer to defend certain research institutes criticized for political bias in the book he was reviewing, even though his own research had been subsidized by those institutes. (If he had admitted to this conflict of interest in the review, he would have been less subject to criticism, but he did not.) The author of a review in the *New England Journal of Medicine* panning a book alleging that environmental chemicals are contributing to an epidemic of cancer was later revealed to be the medical director at chemical producer W. R. Grace & Co., a prime suspect of the industry's critics. This incident occurred in spite of the journal's stated policy that "rather than simply requiring authors to disclose potential conflicts of interest, it would not accept reviews or editorials from anyone connected to firms with a financial stake in the drug or device being discussed" (*San Francisco Chronicle,* December 27, 1997, A3).

Questions concerning special interests, special pleading, and conflict of interest can be highly complex and disputable. Just to determine in a given circumstance what does or does not constitute special pleading or conflict of interest can be a difficult judgment call. Nearly everyone is motivated to some extent by self-interest, and anyone who speaks or writes publicly is likely to have one degree or another of conflict of interest, so the degree of gravity in any particular conflict needs to be evaluated. As a general rule, people should not be criticized as being selfish for arguing in defense of their (or their group's) own right to life, liberty, pursuit of happiness, equality under the law, a living income, or reasonable profit. People *are* subject to criticism, however, (1) if the policy they are arguing for results in them or interests they are speaking for receiving a disproportionate, unfair benefit at the expense of others or of the public interest; or (2) if they cover up or play down their self-interest, pretending to be arguing *disinterestedly* or *impartially* for the public benefits of a policy from which they or their associates will personally benefit.

The **ad hominem** fallacy is a real danger in these matters; that is, you should be careful not to dismiss the substance of someone's arguments *only* because they may be self-interested. Most speakers and writers sincerely believe that what benefits their own group is also in the public interest and that their familiarity with the subject in question qualifies them as authorities; their arguments and evidence always need to be evaluated on their own merits. If special pleading or conflicts of interest are clearly present, however, that should alert you to being extra certain to check out the evidence carefully. It is perfectly legitimate in your writing to point out *possible* conflicts of interest and special pleading in your sources, as one factor among others in evaluating their arguments.

The most honest way of dealing with an unavoidable conflict of interest is to declare it openly and honestly—"full disclosure" is the conventional phrase—and to deal with it as scrupulously as possible. When President George H. W. Bush was making cabinet appointments, he urged nominees to be forthright in avoiding not just actual conflicts but also "any *appearance* of conflict of interest." Judges will sometimes "recuse," or excuse, themselves from sitting in a case in which they have a conflict; legislators will decline to debate or vote on bills involving their own interests; and government appointees will make a full financial disclosure statement. In a controversial case during the administration of President George W. Bush, the Supreme Court was considering a suit filed against Vice President Richard Cheney to make public the records of his private meetings with energy company and foreign oil executives for an energy task force. While this suit was pending, Justice Antonin Scalia flew in Cheney's private plane with him on a duck-hunting trip in Louisiana. However, Scalia refused to recuse himself, scoffing at the suggestion that this trip constituted a conflict of interest. The court ruled in favor of Cheney. When President Obama appointed Elena Kagan to the Supreme Court, Republicans argued, in an analogy with Scalia and Cheney, that she should recuse herself in cases concerning abortion, because she had previously supported pro-choice groups.

As in many semantic issues, even the definition of "special interests" is largely subjective and partisan. Historically, the term has been applied to a few wealthy individuals or businesses trying to buy government favoritism to increase their profits, or to "pork-barrel legislation" (more recently called "earmarks") designed only to benefit some local constituency. In recent years, the original meaning has been dissipated by application of the term (mainly by conservative business interests against their liberal opponents) to any constituency or lobby, no matter how large, and even if not motivated by financial investments. Many advocacy groups are concerned solely with the public good as they view it in principle, without selfish motives, whether on the conservative side like religious and right-to-life groups or on the liberal side like environmentalists, feminists, and pro-choice groups. A second category, including groups like AARP (the American Association of Retired Persons) and the NAACP (National Association for the Advancement of Colored People) certainly represent the special interests of their constituents, but they include millions of diverse members and can generally make a strong case that what is in their interest is also in the public interest.

Conservatives sometimes try to discredit the officials of liberal nonprofit organizations of environmentalists, feminists, consumer advocates, and civil rights activists by claiming that they are in it only for the money they receive in executive salary. However, this line of argument often comes across as ad hominem because those who make it rarely can present any concrete evidence to support it, and they also tend to apply it with **selective vision** that fails to make the same charges against conservative advocacy groups—such as the National Rifle Association, anti-abortion and religious organizations—or against corporate executives, lobbyists, advertising and PR agents, many of whom make a lot more money. (The tax reports of nonprofit organizations are on the public record, so you can research liberal and conservative ones to compare their executive salaries.)

Labor unions are a somewhat more ambiguous case; they undoubtedly lobby for their own financial interests, but they also represent millions of constituents. Critics of unions, though, often accuse their officials of acting in only their own interests, not those of their rank-and-file members, and there are certainly instances of officials defrauding their members. Conservative defenders of business lobbies argue that the owners and executives of corporations likewise represent all their stockholders and employees, as well as the public interest. The credibility of this line of argument was tarnished in 2008 when the reckless profiteering from subprime mortgages by the executives of some of the largest banking and insurance companies precipitated bankruptcies, a stock market crash, and recession. In an earlier cycle of scandals, around 2001, the executives of several huge corporations like Enron enriched themselves by fraudulently inflating the value of company stocks, eventually driving their companies into bankruptcy at the expense of their stockholders and their workers who lost not only their jobs but their pensions invested in the company retirement system.

Another kind of borderline case is the National Rifle Association (NRA), which spends millions annually on lobbying and campaign contributions (see www.opensecrets.org/orgs/summary.php?id=D000000082&lname=National+Rifle+Assn). Officially it is a civil rights organization defending the perceived constitutional rights of its millions of rank-and-file members to bear arms, but it also receives a substantial part of its funding and administration from gun manufacturers and dealers. A skeptical view of NRA's opposition to gun control suggests that manufacturers' and dealers' profits may be a stronger motive than principled defense of Second Amendment rights.

LOBBYING AND PUBLIC RELATIONS

By the earlier definition of propaganda as one-sided information produced by paid professionals, much, if not most, political lobbying and professionally produced public relations are forms of propaganda, although of course there is a wide range in the legitimacy of the interests represented and the validity of the claims made. A vast number of organizations, internationally, nationally, and locally, hire lobbyists and PR representatives: individual corporations and industrial associations, broader groupings like the National Association of Manufacturers and the Chamber of Commerce, professional associations (like the American Medical Association, American Bar Association, and National Education Association), government agencies, foreign governments, trade and public employee unions, and advocacy groups across the political spectrum—environmentalists, the National Rifle Association, religious denominations, retirees, organizations for civil rights and women's rights, groups for or against abortion, and so on.

Opensecrets.org, a project of the nonpartisan Center for Responsive Politics, is an excellent source of up-to-date data on money spent by various forms of liberal and conservative special interests including lobbies, political action committees, and advocacy organizations. Here is their list of the highest-spending lobbies between 1998 and 2012.

Lobbying Client	Total
U.S. Chamber of Commerce	$857,015,680
American Medical Association	$269,507,500
General Electric	$268,810,000
Pharmaceutical Research & Manufacturers of America	$219,393,920
American Hospital Association	$219,214,136
AARP	$214,872,064
Blue Cross/Blue Shield	$186,352,352
National Association of Realtors	$184,433,988
Northrop Grumman	$176,015,253
Exxon Mobil	$173,592,742
Verizon Communications	$168,984,841
Edison Electric Institute	$162,835,999
Business Roundtable	$160,310,000
Boeing Co.	$159,684,310
Lockheed Martin	$154,390,388
AT&T Inc.	$142,039,336
Southern Co.	$134,740,694

General Motors $130,034,170
National Cable & Telecommunications
  Association $127,770,000
Pfizer Inc. $123,827,268

On this list, only the AARP is a citizens' association, representing millions of individual members. All the rest represent corporations or professions and their associations. (Also see the list in Opensecrets.org of the top twenty PACs, five of which are labor unions and the rest corporations and corporate associations.) Making judgments about these diverse groups' motives, methods, and rhetoric calls for nuanced thought, as was indicated earlier with respect to the ambiguity of the definition of a "special interest group." In all corporate and industrial-association lobbies, however, the factor of the profit motive creates a different rhetorical situation from that of nonprofit groups. Both defenders and critics of capitalism agree that the primary purpose of capitalism and corporations is to return maximum profits to stockholders. If this is considered as the first premise in a deductive argument, and if the second premise is that the means of maximizing profits are sometimes contrary to the public interest (e.g., in effects on the environment, workers, consumers, health and safety, or public services like education and communication media), then the conclusion is that at least some corporations are apt to put the quest for profits ahead of the public interest. Corporate executives will rarely admit publicly that they are doing this, however; so much of the lobbying and PR efforts of corporations must consist of propagandistic disguising of selfish interests as public interests.

Another distinguishing factor of corporate lobbying and PR is that large corporations and individuals whose wealth has derived from corporations, whether on the local, national, or international level, generally have more disposable money to spend on PR and advertising than any other interest groups, both on ads for particular products and on advocacy ads promoting their ideological interests; in fact they far outspend all other interest or advocacy groups in this area as well as in political action committees' (PACs) campaign contributions. The only comparable groups are the largest labor unions; however, according to Steve Brouwer's *Sharing the Pie: A Citizen's Guide to Wealth and Power in America,* "In 1996, all labor associations together collected $6 billion in dues, as compared with the $4 trillion in revenues and $360 billion in profits gathered by corporations"—so their relative outlay for lobbying and PR is likely in proportion, though this is a good topic for research. Although the degree of generalization is difficult to call here ("all," "most," "some"?), the combination of the motive to put profits above the public welfare and the wealth to overwhelm opposing interest groups in hiring PR servants is sufficient cause to predict that *a substantial amount* of corporate rhetoric will be propagandistically slanted.

A 1993 article by Joel Bleifuss in *In These Times* was titled "Flack Attack—Public Relations Is Shaping Public Life in Ways We're Not Supposed to Notice." (A "flack" is professional slang for a PR agent; the term connotes someone who will do anything for money.) Bleifuss interviewed John Stauber, editor of the web journal PR Watch and co-author of *Toxic Sludge Is Good for You: Lies, Damned Lies, and the Public Relations Industry*, who said, "Typically a Fortune 500 firm will employ half a dozen PR firms at one time. And the growing trend is one-stop shopping—lobbying, public relations, political consulting, a legal team and a counteractivism grassroots campaign all under one roof." About the last term here, Bleifuss explains, "Sometimes a [corporate or political] PR campaign tries to influence lawmakers covertly, by manufacturing and packaging 'grassroots' expressions of civic outrage and then delivering these messages from the public to elected officials.... This is known as astroturf organizing." In contrast to advertising, in which the sponsor is usually evident, public relations campaigns typically operate secretly; when politicians or media echo messages planted by PR agents, their source is rarely identified or fact-checked. Indeed, invisibility is a point of pride in the profession. Bleifuss says, "The full effect of this corporate propaganda apparatus will never be fully known. It is most successful when the PR professionals leave no tracks near the scene of a winning campaign." If neither individual citizens, grassroots organizations, nor any interest group other than corporations (and some branches of government allied with corporations, like the military) have the resources to counteract the power of corporate lobbying and PR, and if most of us are unaware of the secret workings of those forces, how does that reflect on conservative arguments that those forces are just competing in "the free market of ideas"?

VARIETIES OF PROPAGANDA

"Propaganda" is one of those semantically ambiguous words, with multiple denotations and connotations. Although it usually has a strongly negative connotation, it has one definition that is connotatively neutral, which is simply the propagation of any ideology or viewpoint; in this sense, it is close in meaning to "rhetoric," in the broad sense of persuasion. So in this neutral sense, any individual or group that tries to persuade an audience to its views engages in propaganda and cannot be faulted for doing do.

In the more common, negative sense of the word, propaganda is usually the product of a political or commercial organization that hires professionals to propagate its messages; sometimes one individual who is powerful or wealthy enough to hire others through media ownership or a political organization is the source. It is reasonable to assume that such professionals are not acting primarily out of their own convictions but are flacking for their employers, as a job. When we are evaluating the arguments presented by hired propagandists, it is not necessarily an **ad hominem** or poisoning the well fallacy to point out that they are being paid for making the arguments they do, and therefore that we should be rather skeptical about their validity; at the very least, we need to carefully check out their data and reasoning. Sometimes, however, certain individuals known as ideologues freely choose to be propagandists for a cause or organization out of their own convictions rather than for pay. This situation constitutes a borderline case between the two definitions of propaganda; in such cases, the key question is whether or not these individuals show the other negative traits of propagandists.

These negative traits include those identified by Aldous Huxley in his essay "Propaganda under a Dictatorship," which speaks of "the slogans, the unqualified assertions and sweeping generalizations which are the propagandist's stock in trade."

> "All effective propaganda," Hitler wrote, "must be confined to a few bare necessities and then must be expressed in a few stereotyped formulas." These stereotyped formulas must be constantly repeated, for "only constant repetition will finally succeed in imprinting an idea upon the memory of a crowd."
> ... The demagogic propagandist must therefore be consistently dogmatic. All his statements are made without qualification. There are no grays in his picture of the world; everything is either diabolically black or celestially white. In Hitler's words, the propagandist should adopt "a systematically one-sided attitude towards every problem that has to be dealt with. He must never admit that he might be wrong or that people with a different point of view might be even partially right." (36)

Hitler was an extreme case, but his prescription for propaganda remains depressingly reminiscent of the quadrennial Democratic and Republican nominating conventions and other campaign rallies, TV spectacles stage-managed by entertainment professionals and featuring masses of the faithful chanting platitudinous slogans in much the same manner as Hitler's infamous Nazi Party mass rallies or the brainwashed crowds in Orwell's *1984*. Huxley, incidentally, notes that Hitler claimed to have modeled his rallies on the quasi-militaristic passions stirred up in the spectators at American football games.

One item in propagandists' stock in trade is a mode of **compartmentalization** and selective vision whereby they will predictably accuse their opponents or victims of employing all these traits of one-sided rhetoric that they themselves are employing (while denying that they themselves are using them), in an attempt to obscure the truth by reversing the roles of the honest truth seekers and the propagandists. Watch for examples of this trick in your reading, listening, and viewing of news and opinion media; when you find an example, you can legitimately fault its perpetrator for committing the **tu quoque** ("you too") fallacy—accusing someone else of doing what you yourself are also, or solely, doing.

INVECTIVE AND SMEARING

Chapter 1 concluded with a list of "Ground Rules for Polemicists." It is necessary to clarify the relation of polemics to propaganda, with reference to a third term, *invective*. A polemic is a heatedly partisan argument ("polemics" is the name for this genre of argument and is used as either a singular or plural noun). Invective is a variety of polemics that is abusive and insulting, heavy on name-calling (without sufficient evidence for the names), hyperbolically indignant, simplistically one-sided, and ideologically dogmatic or even fanatic—that is to say, propagandistic. Invective characterizes the rhetoric of many prominent liberals and conservatives alike—think Michael Moore, Bill Maher, and Keith Olbermann versus Ann Coulter, Glenn Beck, and Rush Limbaugh. Journalistic invective is described in terms like a "hatchet job" or "hit piece." So polemics often employ invective and propaganda, but they need not, if they are responsibly reasoned and supported as recommended in "Ground Rules for Polemicists." The calculated use of unscrupulous rhetorical methods by political or other organizations to discredit an opponent, often accompanied by outright malicious lies, is known as "smearing" or "a smear campaign." In a *60 Minutes* interview titled "Confessions of a

Tobacco Lobbyist," former lobbyist Victor Crawford, who was dying of throat cancer from smoking, revealed how he devised a smear campaign against opponents of the tobacco industry in which they were labeled "the health Nazis." Rush Limbaugh has similarly smeared feminists as "feminazis." A frequent, and ugly, variety of smearing in the twentieth century, and one still resorted to by some conservative polemicists today, was known as "red-baiting"—lumping Democrats, liberals, democratic socialists, or social democrats together with Communists in **guilt by association** (disregarding the long history of conflicts, often bloody, among these diverse parties), or discrediting any leftist policy as "communistic." In 2012, Republican Representative Allen West declared at a conservative conference, "I believe there's about 78 to 81 members of the Democrat Party who are members of the Communist Party. It's called the Congressional Progressive Caucus" (*Huffington Post,* April 11, 2012). (West resorted here to the frequent Republican semantic tactic of dropping the *-ic* from the name of the Democratic Party, implying that the party isn't really democratic.)

A form of smear campaign that has become increasingly prominent in recent decades is political negative campaigning and "attack ads," usually on TV and radio. These make malicious accusations, often falsehoods or **half-truths**, against the opposing candidate or position on an initiative and are most effectively timed just before the election, when it is too late for the attacked party to refute them. The political consultants who devise attack ads and other forms of negative campaigning frequently will work for candidates and issues of any party or ideological persuasion, and these consultants have become a class of celebrities in their own right, renowned for their "dirty tricks." They include the late Lee Atwater, who devised the infamous Willy Horton ads for George Bush against Michael Dukakis in the 1988 presidential campaign; Dick Morris, who has represented prominent Republicans as well as President Bill Clinton; and Mary Matalin and James Carville, she a Republican operative and he a Democratic one, married to each other. (See their book *All's Fair* for an entertaining account of political strategizing.)

GOVERNMENT PUBLIC RELATIONS: THE MILITARY-INDUSTRIAL-MEDIA COMPLEX

Various segments of the federal and local governments have researchers and public relations divisions, which are subsidized by our tax dollars. Much, perhaps most, of their activity is conducted in the public interest, simply to collect and convey useful information, and is free of propagandistic motives. In some cases this activity will have an ideological viewpoint that varies according to whether the particular agency tends to be conservative (such as the Defense Department) or liberal (such as the Environmental Protection Agency), and according to the ideology of the party currently in office.

In several ways, the U.S. Department of Defense (DOD), also known as the Pentagon, presents a unique case, along with those areas of the executive branch, primarily the presidency and the Department of State, and of Congress that are closely tied to the DOD. (George Orwell pointed out in his 1947 essay "Politics and the English Language" that the very term "Department of Defense" is a euphemism, since all major world powers, even the most militaristic, had recently adopted that **clean** name instead of the earlier **dirty** one, "Department of War.") On the one hand, nearly everyone agrees that strong military defense is in the public interest. On the other hand, military spending entails several potential conflicts of interest that no other major area of government spending does. First, the defense industry is one of the largest and most profitable in the American private sector, but virtually its only client is the federal government, so military manufacturers maintain well-financed lobbies to win government contracts and maintain their profit levels; this is a prime example of what critics call "corporate welfare" or "socialism for the rich." They are also major campaign contributors, and there is a "revolving door" for executives between the industry and the Defense Department, in what President Eisenhower, a conservative Republican, termed in 1960 (warning against the danger of its growing influence) "the military-industrial complex." Thus there have been periodic scandals concerning bribery in military contracts and grossly inflated DOD expenses, with taxpayers footing the padded bills for items like $900 toilet seats and $100 monkey wrenches. The Iraq war in 2003 was strongly advocated by Vice President Richard Cheney, who had previously been CEO of Halliburton Industries, which became one of the largest military contractors and beneficiaries in that war and which came under attack for gaining contracts with no competitive bidding and for cost overruns and other excess profiteering. Many foreign governments—such as Israel, Saudi Arabia, Kuwait, South Korea, and Taiwan—also have well-financed lobbies in Washington to acquire or maintain American military support, which in turn entails profits for the private companies supplying that support. The American-Israeli Public Affairs Committee—AIPAC—regularly has ranked among the highest-spending lobbies in Washington. Foreign dictators lavishing money in American public relations have been able to turn the heads of some reputable American journalists and scholars toward writing favorably about them, as in the embarrassing case of Libya's Muammar Qaddafi with Benjamin Barber and Joseph Nye, shortly before Qaddafi cracked down brutally against demonstrators for reform and was overthrown (see Jon Wiener, "Professors Paid by Qaddafi," *The Nation,* March 5, 2011).

Another source of potential conflict of interest lies in reporting on American military activity by commercial media that are part of corporate conglomerates whose owners and advertisers include major defense contractors. A prime example was when in the 1991 Gulf War, NBC broadcast glowing reports (subsequently revealed to be false) on the successes of the Patriot missile. Neither NBC nor any other major media mentioned that the electronic components of the missile were manufactured by General Electric, NBC's parent corporation.

One more area of potential conflict of interest has to do with the paradox that much military spending is necessarily invested in costly weapons and personnel that may never be used in a war; the weapons that are never used usually can serve no other purpose and rapidly become obsolete. To a certain extent, this paradox is a necessary evil in maintaining up-to-date weaponry, but a real danger is that the need for the military industry to maintain its profits through constant turnover in weapons, or "planned obsolescence," and for the armed forces to maintain their size and influence, may lead to "the tail wagging the dog," in special pleading by these interests for going to war or at least **appealing to fear** of war for self-serving motives; most of us are highly susceptible to this particular appeal to fear, because as lay people we are dependent on military and political authorities' word that their policies are effective in combating foreign threats. With the end of the Cold War, we might have expected to see a large reduction in American military spending; one possible reason that this did not occur was lobbying by the military industry and DOD to avert having their budgets and profits cut. A central plank in conservatives' ideological platform is opposition to excessive size, bureaucracy, cost, and corruption in federal government agencies. But conservatives are vulnerable to charges of a **double standard** and compartmentalized thinking in their tendency toward promoting constant growth in spending for the Department of Defense without expressing concern about inefficiency there. The key to this inconsistency might be that defense spending also is beneficial to corporate profits—perhaps the highest priority on the conservative ideological agenda, dear to both

Republicans and Democrats dependent on campaign contributions from military contractors and foreign governments that buy American arms or are dependent on American military support.

These are all reasons for remaining aware of the danger that public relations and lobbying by the military-industrial complex may on occasion cross the line from disinterested advocacy in the public interest to propagandistic special pleading and deception. Most governments in most wars through history have tried to cover up their military blunders and atrocities or have fabricated accounts of ones by their enemies. The selling of the Vietnam War to Americans was a prominent example of deception by the government and military brass in our time. More recently, as Bleifuss notes in "Flack Attack," "By the time Reagan left office, 3,000 public relations officers were busy spending $100 million of taxpayers' money annually to manipulate the public's impressions of the military-industrial complex." A classic propaganda campaign described by Bleifuss concerns the Washington PR firm Hill and Knowlton, which in the 1991 Gulf War worked for both the Bush administration and the Kuwaiti royal family (lobbying for American military intervention against Iraq's invasion) to devise a fraudulent atrocity story about Iraqi soldiers pulling babies out of incubators in Kuwait hospitals. This story was highly effective in rallying Americans to war against Saddam Hussein, and when its falsity was revealed, long after the war, no action was taken against its perpetrators. An incident based on this one was depicted in the 1998 film *Wag the Dog,* which satirized a Clintonesque president who starts a phony war to distract public attention from a sex scandal. The film presented a not-very-exaggerated account of the sophistication with which PR consultants can now sell wars like advertisers do soap flakes, tugging on the public's heartstrings with fabricated tales of atrocities by the enemy and heroism by "our boys." (Have you ever heard our enemies' troops referred to as "their boys"?) Again, this is not to imply cynically that reports of American heroism and enemy atrocities are not sometimes truthful—just that they are not *always* true and that a dose of skepticism cannot hurt you.

Hill and Knowlton was again the PR agency of choice for George W. Bush's White House. Stories emerged about a proposed DOD "psychological operations" unit whose job would include disseminating false stories, a plan that was retracted when it became public. (Also see *Weapons of Mass Deception: The Uses of Propaganda in Bush's War on Iraq,* by Sheldon Rampton and John Stauber.) At least five prominent stories about propaganda in the Iraq war have come to light. In one, American news media all showed footage of jubilant

Iraqis pulling down a statue of Saddam Hussein in April 2003. According to a report by David Zucchino in the *Los Angeles Times* (July 3, 2004), that episode was staged by American military officials for the benefit of TV coverage. "A Marine recovery vehicle toppled the statue with a chain, but the effort appeared to be Iraqi-inspired because the psychological team had managed to pack the vehicle with cheering Iraqi children."

A second story was generated by highly publicized news footage, immediately after the initial conquest of Baghdad in spring 2003, of President Bush, dressed in Navy flight gear (as though he had been a combat pilot), landing on an aircraft carrier that had returned from Iraq to San Diego, beneath a banner reading "Mission Accomplished." This episode turned into an embarrassment for Bush after militant resistance to the American occupation escalated.

The third episode concerned Private Jessica Lynch, whose unit in Iraq was ambushed and who was subsequently rescued by U.S. troops from an Iraqi hospital. Initial reports released by the Pentagon included claims that she had been stabbed and shot in hand-to-hand combat, that she was abused in the hospital, and that her rescuers shot their way in against armed resistance. Subsequent revelations cast doubt on all these claims. According to critics of the Pentagon's version, she had not been in combat and her wound resulted from falling from her vehicle, she was well cared for and treated in the hospital, and her rescue was staged as a photo op, with unnecessary gunfire against nonexistent enemy fire. (A BBC reporter called this "one of the most stunning pieces of news management ever conceived.") This was a classic case of "which side are you going to believe?" *People* magazine (June 16, 2003), the source of the BBC quotation, presented an unusually balanced report simply summarizing the opposing accounts. No one doubted the heroism and suffering of Private Lynch, but she herself, when she had recovered enough to speak publicly, was extremely modest and expressed embarrassment over the exaggerated, propagandistic uses that had been made of her ordeal.

In the fourth episode, Army Ranger Pat Tillman, a National Football League player who volunteered for combat duty in Afghanistan, died there in action in 2004. The Pentagon's official account claimed that he was killed by enemy forces, and it took several years for the truth to come out, that he died from our own troops' "friendly fire."

The fifth episode involved dozens of former high-ranking military officers who appear regularly in the media as expert analysts. The *New York Times* reported online (April 20, 2008), "To the public, these men are members of a familiar fraternity, presented tens of thousands of times on television and radio as 'military analysts' whose long service has equipped them to give authoritative and unfettered judgments about the most pressing issues of the post-Sept. 11 world. Hidden behind that appearance of objectivity, though, is a Pentagon information apparatus that has used those analysts in a campaign to generate favorable news coverage of the administration's wartime performance." Furthermore, it is not revealed to the public that these authorities "represent more than 150 military contractors either as lobbyists, senior executives, board members or consultants."

Topics for Discussion and Writing

1. Discuss what kind of conflicts of interest might be present in the topics you study in your major subject.
2. Monitor television, radio, newspaper, and Internet sources of news in your area for possible conflicts of interest stemming from ownership or advertising.
3. If your college or university has an office of research, interview the director and some faculty members conducting sponsored research, and ask them what their policy is for dealing with possible conflicts of interest.
4. If there are any non-university research institutes in your area, interview their administrators and researchers to pose the same question as in number 3.
5. Debate whether the analogy suggested here between Supreme Court justices Scalia and Kagan concerning alleged conflicts of interest is a valid one.
6. Look for examples throughout this book by the author that display the negative traits listed here as characterizing propaganda and invective.
7. In the passage quoted from "Flack Attack," Bleifuss says, "By the time Reagan left office, 3,000 public relations officers were busy spending $100 million of taxpayers' money annually to manipulate the public's impressions of the military-industrial complex." What connotative language does the author use to put a negative spin on the facts he is reporting? Rephrase the sentence in more neutral language, then explain which version you find more persuasive and why. Research the uses of this Pentagon PR budget to determine the extent to which it is or is not a justifiable use of taxpayers' money.
8. "Flack Attack" appeared in *In These Times,* a small-circulation, left-liberal journal of opinion that appears on few newsstands. It was

reprinted in the *Utne Reader,* a digest of left and liberal journals that has a slightly wider circulation. Neither journal has much advertising except for other liberal, nonprofit organizations, which limits financing for wider circulation. To what extent does the scarce coverage of stories like these in the mainstream, commercial media suggest that owners and advertisers have the power to censor news that puts them in a bad light? And to what extent does this form of conservative bias refute conservative claims of liberal bias in mass media?

5

Advertising and Hype

Advertising is such a constant presence in our cultural conditioning, virtually from birth to death, that it is hard for us to view it objectively or critically, and particularly to think of it as a form of propaganda. As with public relations and lobbying, there is of course a huge diversity of sources and motives for advertising. Much advertising, especially on the local level or by nonprofit groups, is straightforwardly informational and honest, and many ads sell products that have a limited target market and features that legitimately distinguish them from their competitors. However, the advertising to which we are most frequently exposed is typically produced to maintain a constant profit level for big businesses that have large, long-range production and sales quotas that depend on artificial stimulation of demand. This kind is produced by hired professional agencies, transmitted through mass media, and characterized by the traits of propaganda identified in Aldous Huxley's account of Hitler's methods: "the systematically one-sided attitude ... the slogans, the unqualified assertions ... confined to a few bare necessities and ... expressed in a few stereotyped formulas."

In Hitler's formula, "only constant repetition will finally succeed in imprinting an idea upon the memory of a crowd." This principle of constant repetition explains what seems to be the senseless, annoying repetition of some television or radio commercials every few minutes—especially in broadcasts of sports events. This and every other aspect of such commercials (as well as many feature films and TV programs) are meticulously calculated through market research, applying the principles of depth psychology, playing on test audiences' subconscious responses; this research has found that when audiences find a commercial annoying, it nevertheless implants the product's name in their minds and they tend to buy it. (Two standard books on psychological manipulation in ads are Vance Packard's *The Hidden Persuaders,* 1957, and Wilson Key's *Subliminal Seduction,* 1974.)

Much of this kind of mass-media advertising is also designed for markets in which there are many competing products that do not differ significantly from one another. As a result many ads cannot tell us anything that really distinguishes the product from others; instead, they employ diverse methods to create a fallacious impression of distinctiveness. Among the most common techniques are

- Emotional, pictorial, or symbolic associations, like the ads set amid rustic greenery or the Wild West—the Marlboro Man, "Like a Rock," and SUVs breaking through wild terrain, though most are driven in cities.
- The slogan: "Fly the Friendly Skies," "Nobody Does It Like You."
- The dramatized pseudo-debate ("Tastes great." "Less filling.").
- The corporate image that gives the illusion of a friendly, personal identity to impersonal corporations (the GEICO gecko, Betty Crocker, Colonel Sanders, "the Microsoft Family," nationwide restaurant chains like Cracker Barrel that imitate the old-fashioned, local country restaurant).
- The celebrity endorsement, which implies that the authority of some sports or entertainment star who has no special knowledge about the field of the endorsed product, and who is being paid a large amount to endorse it, should make you want to buy this brand rather than another.

Perhaps the most influential means of creating the illusion of difference between essentially indistinguishable products is the prestige accorded to brand names themselves. The culturally conditioned assumption is that the familiar brand is likely to be superior to the unfamiliar one. Does the familiarity of brand names, however, mean anything more than that the corporations producing them can afford to spend a great deal of money to establish that familiarity? "As Seen on TV" on a package just means that the manufacturer has paid to advertise the product. So reliance on brand names is a case of the causal fallacy that social critic and historian Daniel Boorstin, in his 1961 book *The Image: A Guide to Pseudo-Events in America,* calls a "self-fulfilling prophecy." Boorstin argues that celebrity is a form of self-fulfilling prophecy because "the celebrity is a person who is known for his well-knownness" (57), without regard for the quality of whatever achievement has brought him or her public recognition. Likewise, advertised brands are famous mainly *because they are advertised*. Celebrities themselves become products, their fame marketed by advertising and public relations agencies.

Maybe we are better off buying a brand that we know is an established one rather than one that we've never heard of and that might be a fly-by-night product. By the same token, however, brand-name manufacturers have been known to market shoddy products, either through complacency over public trust in their brands or through exploitation of that trust. Brand-name products are also likely to be more expensive than non-branded ones, because the expense of advertising is added to the sale price. Generic products exactly the same as brand-name ones are now widely available for a lower price.

One defense of commercial sponsorship of radio and television programs is that the revenue it provides gives us free access to the programs. Still, the money that this system costs us in the additional price we pay for advertised products might conceivably, as in some other countries, go into a corporate tax that would fund public, commercial-free broadcasting, thus also removing control by sponsors over programming.

ARE YOU TAKEN IN BY ADS?

You might firmly believe that you are not "taken in" by advertising, or media messages in general, but how do you know that you do not unconsciously absorb many culturally conditioned assumptions through the media, and particularly the inescapable flooding of consciousness by millions of ads—many of them calculated for subconscious influence? Consider the universal phenomenon of young people, many of whom doubtless claim they aren't influenced by advertising, wearing clothes that are not only the most-advertised name brands but also prominently display the manufacturer's logo. Isn't it a strange culturally conditioned assumption that we should pay money to turn ourselves into a free, walking ad for Nike or Tommy Hilfiger?

A contrary view that has received a lot of attention in recent media scholarship cites evidence that audiences are often capable of seeing through and resisting the ideological messages sent out by the media or of re-appropriating those messages to their own purposes. Conservatives have traditionally made this argument in defense of "the free market of ideas" and consumers' "freedom to choose," and they point to instances in which high-powered advertising campaigns have failed. (A contrary argument is that advertising is obviously successful in enough instances to warrant companies' investing constantly increasing billions in it every year.) Some critics with liberal-populist views have also made the same argument to show the power of the common people to resist corporate manipulation. This is always a lively topic for writing or class discussion; can you and your classmates think of more examples in which you, and the public in general, have been swayed by advertising, or in which advertising has been resisted?

POLITICAL AND ADVOCACY ADVERTISING

In recent decades, political advertising has become the tail that wags the dog of American politics. The amount spent on advertising, primarily on television, has escalated so much that it has taken up the largest share of campaign contributions and given an ever-greater advantage to wealthy candidates and to corporate and other wealthy contributors, as well as the biggest labor unions, who in return are likely to expect favorable legislation from the candidates and policies they have backed. Most other democratic countries restrict the amount of television advertising allowed and money spent on it and in some cases have required that free equal time be made available to opponents.

Consider the absurd increase in the length of political campaigns, as presidential candidates begin virtually on one election day to run for the next one four years later, while the primary season drags out for a year before the general election as states compete to have the earliest primary, to which candidates and media alike will flock. The prime beneficiaries here are parties and individuals who can raise the most money to outlast rivals and who have constantly increased the stakes in campaign financing, mainly from corporate-wealthy patrons. However, the news media are equally complicit, through the billions of profits they now generate from both campaign advertising and the bump in general advertising for coverage of these protracted campaigns. Further beneficiaries are the star TV reporters, commentators (whether conservative or liberal), and debate moderators who now earn millions thanks to the boom in advertising. So news media themselves have developed a conflict of interest against placing campaign finance reform on the agenda of media attention.

In 2010 the U.S. Supreme Court reversed a long-standing law with a controversial ruling in the Citizens United case that allows corporations and labor unions to make direct contributions to campaigns and parties, or to sponsor political ads, without identifying themselves as the funder. This ruling led to an even greater proliferation of the long-established custom of special interests disguising themselves in campaign or issue-advocacy ads as nonpartisan citizens' organizations, comparable to the "front groups" used by the Communist Party internationally in the mid-twentieth century. (No, this is not red-baiting guilt by association—only an analogy between the use of front groups on the left and right.) So The Coalition to Protect Seniors, which ran ads opposing President Obama's health insurance bill, was secretly a front for private health insurers like Blue Cross, Aetna, and United Healthcare (Mike McIntire, "The Secret Sponsors," *New York Times Week in Review,* October 3, 2010, 1). Patients United Now, another group advertising against Obama's bill, was a spin-off of Citizens for a Sound Economy, as was Americans for Prosperity, a group that advocates limited government and opposes climate-change legislation. All three of these organizations and several similar ones funding conservative causes like the Tea Party movement were created by David and Charles Koch, Kansas billionaires who own Koch Industries, which produces pharmaceuticals, chemicals, natural gas, fertilizers, and other products whose profits would be affected by regulatory legislation (Michael Tomasky, "Something New on the Mall," *New York Review of Books,* October 22, 2010, 6; see also the discussion of EnergyTomorrow.org in Chapter 6). Liberal forces like labor unions and environmentalists also spend a great deal on advocacy advertising and campaign contributions, but they arguably more often identify themselves directly, which you can verify for yourself. Especially after the Citizens United decision, there was some movement in Congress toward laws requiring fuller disclosure of who is funding political ads and campaign contributions, though neither this movement nor one to curtail campaign spending or political ads on TV stood much chance of overcoming opposition by those of either major party who got elected through the present system. Nor was much support for disclosure laws to be expected from news media corporations that have been enriched from the escalation in campaign and advocacy advertising.

The main rhetorical issue involved in restricting political advertising is whether, as conservatives argue, advertising and particularly political advertising are constitutionally protected modes of free speech. (Conservatives make the same argument in opposition to limiting campaign contributions.) The liberal rebuttal is that the principle of the First Amendment guarantee of free speech was to protect unpowerful individuals and small groups against government censorship, not to allow wealthy corporate interests to monopolize public communication.

FOOD AND CHILDREN'S ADVERTISING

Most of us lack adequate knowledge about the food we eat daily, and this is perhaps the most glaring instance of the need for consumer education that delves beneath the surface of the advertising and marketing that we are inundated with. Several recent books, including Eric Schlosser's *Fast Food Nation* and Michael Pollan's *The Omnivore's Dilemma,* present exposés of the practices of corporate food producers that are often shockingly irresponsible in concern for nutrition, inhumane toward their employees and toward animals raised for food, and environmentally disastrous. (A Hollywood film of *Fast Food Nation* skillfully fictionalized that nonfiction book, through a graphic dramatization of its themes.)

Consumer-advocacy organizations like the Center for Science in the Public Interest (CSPI) are also good sources of information on deceptive practices in food marketing. One CSPI article, "Ten Food Secrets You Should Know," pointed out, "A large bucket of unbuttered popcorn at theaters (like United Artists) that pop in coconut oil has almost three days' worth of artery-clogging fat! Add the fake 'butter' and you'll boost the cholesterol-raising fat to almost four days' worth. That's like eating *eight* McDonald's Big Macs." And, "Haagen-Daz has managed to squeeze in more than twice the fat of regular ice cream, like Breyers.... A cup of Chocolate Chocolate Chip has as much saturated fat (24 grams) as three McDonald's Quarter Pounders."

In a syndicated column titled "Children Now Facing Adult Health Issues," Joan Ryan related the following:

- Children watching television during Saturday mornings view more than twice as many advertisements for unhealthy foods as adults see during programs aired after 9 p.m.
- The average American child sees 10,000 food commercials each

year. Ninety-five percent are for fast food, sugary cereals, soft drinks, and candy.
- The entire government budget for nutritional education is one-fifth the annual advertising budget for Altoid mints.
- The number of severely overweight children in the United States has doubled since 1980. Nationally, hospital costs related to childhood obesity have more than tripled in the past 20 years to $127 million, says the Centers for Disease Control and Prevention.

Ryan uses the analogy of cigarette advertising having been banned on TV and radio in arguing that junk-food advertising for children should also be banned, and she cites several other democracies that have in fact banned it. The rationale for such a ban is that children have not developed the reasoning capacities or acquired the information necessary to be "free to choose" at the level of adults.

ADVERTISING SELLS MORE THAN PRODUCTS

In several ways the social influence of advertising extends beyond the influence of this or that ad for this or that product. The propagandistic, "systematically one-sided attitude," as Huxley puts it, in ads consists of their telling us only positive things about both the product and the company manufacturing it while suppressing anything negative about either. In this sense, the huge portion of mass communication dominated by corporate advertising can be considered detrimental to the constitutional principle of freedom of the press. Consider how different our thinking about advertised products might be if print and broadcast media allowed free equal time for critics of every product advertised to point out its possible unhealthy, unsafe, or environmentally destructive aspects, or to examine its manufacturer's political, labor, and financial practices, for example, its lobbying and campaign contributions, use of sweatshops, or union busting.

While every product ad is also an indirect form of propaganda for the manufacturer, other varieties of ads are direct forms of corporate propaganda. One is institutional ads designed as public relations for a company, such as those familiar to viewers of the *News Hour* on PBS for "Archer-Daniels-Midland, Supermarket to the World," an agricultural-chemical and ethanol manufacturer that has been convicted of price-fixing and charged with buying political influence through campaign contributions. Other forms of corporate propaganda include public service announcements (PSAs), designed as statements in the public interest, which do not promote sales for the sponsor but do promote its public relations, and advocacy ads, discussed above, that represent the interests of a single company or association of companies on public issues, such as those on energy or environmental policies that are sponsored by oil companies or consortiums of producers like the American Petroleum Institute.

Critics of these practices do not deny that corporations have the right to engage in all of them. The cause for criticism is that big businesses are able to exert inequitable influence on public discourse because their available funds for advertising and public relations far exceed those of all other interest groups such as unions and nonprofit consumer-advocacy and environmentalist organizations like Public Citizen, Common Cause, People for the American Way, and the Sierra Club. These groups do sponsor some advertising and public relations for their own causes, but much less than corporations because nonprofits derive income primarily from dues and contributions from members; their budgets are quite small in comparison to major corporations' profit-derived advertising, lobbying, and PR budgets. The basic fact that the media are owned by corporations for commercial purposes works against their receptivity to messages critical of corporations or capitalism. To imagine some degree of parity with commercial media, we would need to envision a TV or radio network or weekly magazine with the circulation of *USA Today* or CNN devoted explicitly to the viewpoint of labor unions, consumer-advocacy and environmentalist groups, or socialists. Why do you think no such media exist?

Another sense in which ads sell more than particular products is that the whole system of commercial advertising promotes consumerism and materialism, a value system in which people are conditioned to regard consuming commodities as one of the most important things in their lives—more important, say, than their role as citizens or virtuous individuals. (Note that this sense of the word "consumerism" is different, indeed opposite, from the sense of the word identified with consumer advocacy.) The culturally conditioned assumption is that our social identity should be primarily that of passive, uncritical consumers (of both products and politics), not that of active, critical citizens.

Finally, every commercial ad is also, implicitly, an ad for the whole system of commercial advertising and its essential role in the capitalist economy. So the millions of ads that inundate us all enforce the culturally conditioned assumptions of the free enterprise system, as opposed to socialism or a social-democratic mixed economy.

HYPE

How many times have you looked forward keenly to a movie or TV program, a sports event, a concert or recording, a restaurant meal, or a travel experience, then felt let down afterward, asking yourself, in the refrain of an old popular song, "Is that all there is?" Advertising and public relations agents use the noun *hype* or the verb *to hype* as synonyms for a sales or publicity promotion, especially in show business, but the phrase also often implies hyperbolic exaggeration or the buildup of "extravagant expectations," in the words of Daniel Boorstin in *The Image*. Hype exploits our wishes that our life can be like the fantasy world depicted in the media, where everyone is young, beautiful, slender, smiling, and leads a carefree lifestyle—and it implicitly tells us that we can attain that world by buying the expensive commodities advertised in the media. Travel hype entices us with pictures of glamorous resorts and cruises, isolated tropical beaches, and romantic couples hugging beneath warm waterfalls. But when we get to our dream destination we are likely to find the resorts and cruises populated mainly by elderly retirees, the beaches mobbed with fellow tourists blaring loud music, the waterfalls inaccessible except by helicopter or filled with sharp, slippery rocks and their water too cold to bear.

To further understand the reasons for hype in mass culture, it is necessary to realize that, for example, television and radio stations broadcast virtually all day every day, while newspapers, magazines, and web journals need to publish at about the same length every issue, so each medium must come up with enough material to fill the time or space between the advertisements they have sold and to attract the audience to the ads, which provide most of their revenue. Consequently, much of their content is just filler, and they are constantly building up excessive expectations of what we will be getting out of their productions, the commodities their advertisers are selling, and, indeed, life in general. This kind of hype has accelerated more than ever with the expansion of cable television broadcasts, especially full-time news channels like CNN, MSNBC, and Fox News and sports channels like ESPN. The news channels compete with one another in sensation seeking, blowing trivial events out of proportion, and in constant, superficial "analysis" by hammy performer-pundits (while evading the in-depth analysis of serious issues that such expansion could facilitate).

Cognitive overload as a form of hype in current society is most prominent in the saturation of young and old alike by televised and other distractions, their sound-bite sensationalism, and their assault on the public attention span, most recently manifested in students' constant cell-phone conversations and text-messaging, when they are not plugged into their iPods or devoting hours per day to computer or video games, Facebook, and Twitter. It has become nearly impossible to escape blaring music in any public space in the world, drowning out the possibility for conversation or contemplation. When I ask my students whether they are ever bothered by this noise in restaurants and bars, they say they just take it for granted, and they are taken aback to learn that it is the product of market research showing that the louder and more constantly music plays, the more alcohol customers buy. In the totalitarian societies of both Huxley's *Brave New World* and Orwell's *1984,* solitude and individual thought are stigmatized and prevented by similar constant noise and group distractions.

In TV sports coverage, think about how little air time is devoted to actual depiction of play and how much time to redundant play-by-play narration (a holdover from the age of radio when the audience couldn't see the action), hysteria-pitched commentary, dramatic musical overlays, interviews with athletes laboring the obvious (the essence of sports, after all, is performance, not analysis of that performance), and the ever proliferating commercials. Even actual sports events like major league baseball games are now hyped up with high-decibel music between innings, electronically prompted cheers, and high-tech scoreboard spectacles.

In the same way that drug addicts need ever-escalating fixes as their systems become accustomed to the previous level, audience members are perceived by media producers to become saturated with a certain level of coverage and so to need ever-increasing doses in order to keep ratings from falling. Another major cause for media hype is the constant escalation of corporate advertising, which necessitates accompanying increases in TV programming. Take, for example, the expansion of professional sports teams and seasons over recent decades, driven mainly by advertisers' quest for bigger audiences and by broadcasters' quest for increased advertising revenue. In baseball, the American and National leagues used to contain eight teams each; the 154-game season ended in September, with a one-game play-off in case of a tie, followed by the World Series the first week in October.

Little by little the leagues have expanded (at last count) to three five-team divisions in each league. The season by 2011 lasted 166 games, followed by two sets of play-offs before the World Series, including second-place "wildcard" teams—and in 2012 yet another wildcard winner was added in each league. Even the play-offs have expanded from one to three to five to seven games, so that the season stretches nearly to November, overlapping with football and basketball to create a mind-numbing overload of sports and attendant hype.

Then there is holiday hype, especially surrounding Christmas, driven by the always-accelerating quest for corporations to transform the traditional spirit of holidays into sales campaigns. The Christmas sales season used to begin the day after Thanksgiving, but it now begins as early as October. Christmas carols and seasonal songs may be appealing the first few times we hear them every year in stores and in the media, but their repetition hundreds of times over is enough to make us sick of them. The commercial pressure to buy expensive gifts for all one's family and friends—which are often unneeded and unwanted and which put many buyers into heavy debt—amounts to extortion, as does the pressure to spoil children with a glut of presents unequaled in any past historical time. Likewise for the excessive expectations fostered by media images of holiday jollity and family companionship, which pressure people into feelings of guilt if they and their families do not live up to them, to the point where the holidays often actually exacerbate family frictions. Treatment for depression and other mental illness spikes at Christmastime, as do hospital emergency room crises.

Topics for Discussion and Writing

1. Watch an hour or so of TV commercials and decide how many of them tell you anything concrete about the product that substantially distinguishes it from competing brands. Evaluate the general quality of the reasoning in the various ads. Are any of them selling something beyond the product itself, as described in this chapter? Write counter-commercials for any that you find deceptive about the product, the company manufacturing it, or the broader ideas it promotes.
2. Other democracies place stricter limits on televised political advertising on TV and radio than the United States does, because its expense favors wealthier parties and candidates. Debate the pros and cons of the constitutional and practical issues here, and do some research on other countries' policies.

3. When you see ads sponsored by "Citizens for ..." or "Americans United Against ... ," do an Internet search for who is behind them. First find their web home page, then look for a link to "About Us," "Who We Are," or "Board of Directors." That should provide clues to what special interests the organization may be a front for, whether it has a liberal or conservative agenda, and whether it is more inclined to support Democrats or Republicans.
4. Concerning the issues raised in "Ten Food Secrets You Should Know" and "Children Now Facing Adult Health Issues," to what extent does the lack of public knowledge about such facts refute arguments that consumers are free to "take or leave" advertised products or that advertising is just part of the free exchange of ideas under the constitutional principle of freedom of speech? How different do you think consumer attitudes would be if commercials and print ads were regularly followed by information like this? Discuss why this would or would not be feasible. How many of your classmates have taken courses in high school or college that provide this kind of consumer information? Debate why there should or should not be more such courses.
5. "Ten Food Secrets You Should Know" itself appeared in a mail ad for the Center for Science in the Public Interest soliciting membership and subscriptions for the newsletter of this nonprofit, liberal research institute, a Naderite consumer-advocacy organization. Is advertising for such a purpose substantially different from the commercial advertising it is meant to counteract in the motives of its sponsors, writers, publishers, or broadcasters?
6. Review the points made in "Children Now Facing Adult Health Issues"; what arguments for and against banning cigarette or children's junk-food advertising in broadcast and other media can be made? Is there a possible slippery slope fallacy involved in these arguments? Once certain kinds of advertising are banned, can we draw the line about what others should be?
7. What examples in current culture can you think of that illustrate Boorstin's terms "extravagant expectations," "pseudo-events," and "self-fulfilling prophecies"? Debate the sections here on "cognitive overload," sports, and holiday hype, whether, for example, the constant expansion of sports leagues and seasons, for the primary purpose of increased television broadcasting and advertising revenue, has been a good or a bad thing for sports.

6

Analyzing Economic Arguments and Statistical Trickery

This chapter will apply critical analysis of economic arguments to one of the most important debates in recent decades between conservatives and liberals or leftists—the extent to which economic inequalities, and especially the gap between the rich and the middle class and poor, have been increasing in the United States since the 1970s. This debate also involves the consequences for economic inequality of tax cuts and cutbacks in government regulation of business, which were justified by "supply-side economics," or "Reaganomics," during the presidential administration of Ronald Reagan (1980–1988) and again revived by President George W. Bush (2000–2008), by John McCain as a presidential candidate in 2008, and Mitt Romney in 2012; throughout both of his terms, President Obama clashed with Republicans in Congress over his attempts to rescind President Bush's tax cuts for the rich and to restore more regulation of business. Conservative and liberal positions on these issues are more fully developed in "An Outline of Conservative and Liberal or Leftist Arguments . . ." at the end of this chapter, and it would be helpful for you to read through them now as background for the following discussion of statistical evidence presented by the opposing sides in support of their general lines of argument.

Here are some preliminary points to keep in mind. First, these are not just abstract matters of economics but crucial facts of life for you and every individual, directly pertinent to your own financial future. These facts include the availability and cost to students of tax-funded, public secondary, college, and graduate education (and of student financial aid), what jobs will be available to you after graduation and how much they pay, what your tax burden will be in relation to that of wealthy people and corporations, how much government deficits cost you in taxes, whether Social Security and Medicare will still be funded when you are old enough to receive them, and whether adequate health insurance for all Americans would be a possibility if priorities in taxation and areas of government spending were changed.

Also keep in mind the different levels of audience at which arguments on these issues, based largely on statistics, are pitched. The highest level is that of specialized economic analysis, which can get too advanced for nonspecialists like most of us to evaluate, and which is developed in scholarly or professional articles, reports, and books that are too long to include in a textbook like this. So why should we even dare to delve into issues whose resolution might only be found in texts that are over our heads? One answer is that even at that level, there are fierce disagreements and polemical battles between conservative and liberal economists. Another answer is that scholarly discourse on these issues gets popularized at the level of mass media, in political speeches and in op-ed columns, which are presumably comprehensible to general readers or listeners. That is the level we will be studying here, with analysis of them that relies mainly on unspecialized, commonsense reasoning. The sound-bite length and lack of documentation in such articles limits their value, but they can be useful in introducing lines of argument and, at best, citing sources that we can pursue in research from there. Some citations and links will be included here for longer, more scholarly versions of liberal versus conservative lines of argument.

Finally, keep in mind that the polemics on these issues are a classic case of how opposing forces try to control the rhetorical and semantic agenda. In that effort, liberals predictably accuse conservative spokespeople of being paid propagandists for the rich, while conservatives accuse liberal ones, especially academic ones like me, of **special pleading** on behalf of tax-funded government spending that provides their jobs, at least in public schools and colleges, and on behalf of the labor unions they belong to.

TAX POLICY AND THE WEALTH GAP

Clear opposition on these issues appeared in op-ed columns in the *Los Angeles Times,* "The Rich Aren't Made of Money," by Jonah Goldberg (November 17, 2007), and "A Very Special Kind of Math," by Jonathan Chait (April 29, 2005). Goldberg is an editor of the conservative *National Review* and author of *Liberal Fascism: The Secret History of the American Left: From Mussolini to the Politics of Meaning.* Chait is an editor of the liberal-to-conservative *New Republic* and author of *The Big Con: The True Story of How Washington Got Hoodwinked and Hijacked by Crackpot Economics.*

Goldberg defends then-President George W. Bush's tax cuts for the wealthiest Americans against Democrats' opposition: "According to Democrats, it's greedy to want to keep your own money, but it's 'justice' to demand someone else's." He asserts, "The top 1% of wage-earners already provide nearly 40% of federal income tax revenues. And the bottom half of taxpayers contribute only about 3%." He makes an emotional appeal on behalf of the rich: "We treat the rich like a constantly regenerating piñata, as if they will never change their behavior no matter how many times they get whacked by taxes."

Although Chait's column appeared two years earlier, it refutes this line of argument made by many conservatives before and after Goldberg, in which the fallacy is claiming to "measure the fairness of a tax code by looking at what share of the taxes various groups pay without considering how much they earn." When President Reagan was elected in 1980, the rate for the top income tax bracket was 70 percent (on income over some $300,000 a year, though the rate on any individual's income was lower on amounts up to that level). Under Reagan and succeeding presidents that rate has been cut, currently by half, to 35 percent. (President Clinton raised it to about 39 percent, but Bush cut that back, and President Obama attempted to return to Clinton's level.) Simply as a problem in deductive logic, how is it possible for the tax rate to have been cut in half for the upper bracket but for its individual members to be paying more tax dollars? Chait provides one obvious answer: "The top 0.1% are paying a higher share of the tax burden because their share of the national income is rising faster than their tax rates are falling.... In 1979, the highest-earning 0.1% took home about 3% of the national income, and paid about 5% of the taxes. In 1999, they earned about 10% of the national income and paid about 11% of the taxes." (The increasing *number* of rich people has also increased their tax share as a group—although analysts are sometimes ambiguous about whether they are discussing individual or collective gains within a class.)

Conversely, Goldberg says, "The top 1% of wage earners already provide nearly 40% of federal tax revenues. And the bottom half of taxpayers contribute only about 3%." If the income for the bottom 50 percent had also increased at anything like the rate of the top 1 percent, we can deduce that they too would be paying more in taxes even after tax-rate reductions. But since they are paying comparatively *less* as a group, isn't the logical inference that they must be *earning* less? (Much empirical evidence presented by liberals indicates that the middle and lower classes have indeed lost ground in income and net worth.)

In this perspective, it becomes apparent that arguments by Goldberg and many other conservatives contain a large element of statistical and semantic slanting, framing, or "spin." Conservatives typically use phrases like "the burden of taxation has shifted increasingly to the rich," with the connotation that the wealthy are suffering and have been forced to take over the cost of taxation from the slackers who don't pay their share (in reality, as noted above, because they *make* less). Another common line is that high taxes "penalize" the rich and rob them of their incentive. Elementary logic, however, would seem to dictate that under just about any democratic system or degree of taxation, the more money people make, the larger the share of taxes they will pay. This would hold true even under the flat tax system favored by many conservatives (where all income brackets pay at the same rate) or the "Fair Tax" system advocated by many conservative leaders, a form of flat-rate national sales tax. It is all the more true if the relative share of income gained by the rich is constantly increasing while that of the middle class and poor is decreasing. If Bill Gates made all the income in America, he'd also be paying all the income taxes. Would this be a "burden" and a "penalty"? Chait suggests that conservatives sometimes seem to insinuate—without making it explicit—that the more money people have, the less they should be expected to pay in taxes, while the less money people have, the more they should be expected to pay.

Goldberg downplays the escalation of wealth in the past few decades at the level of *Forbes 400* billionaires and multimillion-dollar CEO salaries. Nor does he acknowledge the simultaneous cutting of income taxes in half for this income level since 1980, or comparable reductions in corporate, capital gains, and estate taxes. (See, among others, David Cay Johnston, *Perfectly Legal: The Covert Campaign to Rig Our Tax System to Benefit the Super Rich—and Cheat Everybody Else*. Johnston also argues that some taxes that are hardest on the middle class and poor, especially payroll deductions for Social Security and Medicare, have stealthily been raised to offset cuts in income tax, as Goldberg also obliquely implies.) The issue that provoked Goldberg's column at the beginning is simply the opposition by Democrats to *further* cuts at this level and the statement by an economic adviser to Obama that "multibillion-dollar hedge fund managers" can afford to have their tax cuts rolled back by 5 percent without pain. So is Goldberg perhaps being hyperbolic to characterize these modest proposals with invective like "pumped for as much cash as we need"? ("We" is implicitly "un-rich America," which "mugs rich America.") To be sure, Chait indulges in similar invective and ridicule of conservative thinkers here and more so in *The Big Con*, and once again, we should judge the worth of invective on either side on how well it is supported with reasoning and evidence.

Goldberg and other conservatives might also be employing a slippery slope fallacy in which any effort by liberals to return tax levels for the rich closer to their level in America a mere three decades ago, or to stem the extreme increase in economic inequality, is demonized with slogans like "class warfare" and "confiscation." As a presidential candidate in 2008, Barack Obama advocated restoring taxes to their level in Bill Clinton's presidency, only 4 percent higher than at present. A letter in the *Knoxville News-Sentinel* in 2008 quoted Obama as saying, "'A strong government hand is needed to assure that income is distributed more equitably.' This is Marxist. Vote for Obama? No thank you." Does wanting to reduce income inequality to its level in America eight or thirty years earlier, or prevent its further escalation, make one a Marxist? "Wealth redistribution" is used as a scare word by conservatives, but what do you think they would say in response to the substantial evidence that in the past three decades wealth in America has been redistributed from the poor and middle class to the rich?

In a column titled "What's Behind Income Disparity?" (*Washington Post*, September 27, 1993), conservative George Will wrote,

> A society that values individualism, enterprise and a market economy is neither surprised nor scandalized when the unequal distribution of marketable skills produces large disparities in the distribution of wealth. This does not mean that social justice

must be defined as whatever distribution of wealth the market produces. But it does mean that there is a presumption in favor of respecting the market's version of distributive justice. Certainly there is today no prima facie case against the moral acceptability of increasingly large disparities of wealth.

By this Will seems to assert that increasing inequality is good for society. Would a logical implication of this assertion be that the more inequality increases, the better? Do Will, Goldberg, or other conservatives give any indication of where they would draw the line at a point past which increasing inequality would be bad for American society? (You might read some of Will's more recent columns or books to see if he has clarified or modified his position.) It is fair play for conservatives to ask liberals where *they* would draw the line past which decreasing inequality would be bad for society. However, most influential liberal sources on economics are pretty clear in advocating that tax rates, regulation of business, and real wages just be returned to their level in 1980 before the advent of Reaganomics.

Goldberg and other conservatives further semantically "frame" the whole concept of taxation negatively, tarring allegedly liberal beliefs about taxes with **dirties** like "anything left after Uncle Sam picks your pockets is a gift," "covetousness as social policy," "government as 'an extortionist,'" and "it's greedy [for conservatives?] to want to keep your own money, but it's 'justice' [for liberals?] to demand someone else's." Liberals, however, have quite a different conception of taxation, and if they were able to frame the public discussion of the issue, it would go something like the following:

> First, taxes are not "extortion" by the government but simply the operating costs we should be happy to pay for all the benefits we expect from government. Conservatives resort to an irrational **appeal to fear** of government that fails to recognize that in American democracy, government serves the people, not vice versa. Government policies on taxation and other issues are ultimately subject to the people's will, and if the people fail to curb the government in excessive taxation, that is no one's fault but their own, so conservatives should be blaming the majority of voters instead of making government the scapegoat.
>
> Second, in the liberal view, the justifications for progressive taxation are (1) that those in the highest bracket can afford to pay higher taxes because their after-tax, disposable income and net worth are still far above their basic living expenses, in contrast to the middle class and poor, for whom taxes come out of income

that is barely, if at all, sufficient to meet basic expenses; (2) that progressive taxes also help to keep the gap in wealth—and, more importantly, power—between the rich and everyone else from growing ever wider; and (3) that it is the rich, not the lower-class recipients of welfare and other "entitlements," who benefit most from government spending, e.g., defense and aerospace contracts, "corporate welfare," bailouts of failing industries like banking and mortgages in the 2000s, and the millions spent by public agencies like schools and colleges providing jobs and purchasing private-sector equipment, construction, and services. Likewise for the services funded by taxes like public education, which trains the corporate workforce and enables workers to earn enough money to buy commodities, thus keeping up the level of corporate profits; services like law enforcement, which protects the wealthy from theft or physical attack and maintains the social stability that allows prosperity; and above all national defense, which protects the corporate and personal possessions of the wealthy from being destroyed or confiscated by foreign invaders. The "free market" economy would probably collapse if it were not for the employment, spending, and education provided by the public sector.

These arguments tend to be suppressed by conservative polemicists, who for the past three decades have waged an unrelenting campaign against government spending (except for the military), a campaign that, according to liberal *New York Times* columnist Paul Krugman, they call "starve the beast." In *The Great Unraveling*, Krugman quotes Republican strategist Grover Norquist as saying he wants to shrink government "down to the size where we can drown it in the bathtub" (xxi–xxii)—leaving corporations and the rich in uncontested control of society.

Thomas Frank's 2008 book *The Wrecking Crew: How Conservatives Rule* more fully develops Krugman's claim about Norquist's and allied Republicans' hidden agenda of budget cuts as a strategy for defeating liberal constituencies that benefit from government funding and regulation. Frank quotes passages written by Norquist that reflect his express aim to "crush the structures of the left," including labor unions, public schools and universities, welfare, Social Security and Medicare (whose administration would be turned over to corporations for profit), and trial lawyers who defend plaintiffs in damage suits against corporations (258).

If conservatives want to refute these arguments, they need to address them directly instead of resorting to straw man distortions and red-herring distractions.

So in researching conservative sources, see if you can find ones that do directly refute any of these arguments. Arthur Laffer, one of the original theoreticians of Reaganomics in the 1980s, wrote an extensive rebuttal to Chait's *The Big Con*, at the level of advanced economics, published in *National Review Online*. (Also see Chait's article about Laffer, "Feast of the Wingnuts," and responses from conservatives in *New Republic Online*, September 10, 2007.)

Another semantic topic, unconcretized verbal abstractions, is pertinent here. The *Wall Street Journal* editorialized (November 13, 2007) against politicians who "want to raise taxes and other government obstacles to the kind of risk-taking and hard work that allow Americans to climb the income ladder so rapidly." George Will's "What's Behind Income Disparity?" similarly justified increasing concentration of wealth at the top because it is necessary to "a high rate of savings—the deferral of gratification that makes possible high rates of investment in capital, research and development and education," and he concluded, "That is why promoting more equal distribution of wealth might not be essential to, or even compatible with, promoting a more equitable society. And why increasingly unequal social rewards can conduce to a more truly egalitarian society, one that offers upward mobility equally to all who accept its rewarding disciplines." All this is at a rather high level of abstraction and prompts the questions in our Rhetoric Checklist #13, about theory versus practice: "Are the ... abstract principles consistent with empirical (verifiable) facts and probabilities, and are they based on adequate firsthand witness to the situation in question?" The ideal conservative model is the entrepreneur who "defers gratification," scrimping and saving to risk her or his own capital and borrowed funds, to start a business introducing an innovative, socially beneficial product or service that also creates jobs, and who works hard building up and personally managing the business day by day, year after year, until it is profitable. There are unquestionably many such entrepreneurs.

But if we look at current lists of big financial winners, we also see many who fit quite a different profile. Leftist columnist Holly Sklar says about the 2007 *Forbes* magazine's list of the 400 wealthiest Americans, "Nearly half of the 45 new members made their fortunes in hedge funds and private equity. Money manager John Pearson joins the list after pocketing more than $1 billion short-selling subprime credit." (Subprime credit involves bonds based on high-risk loans whose proliferation led to the mortgage meltdown of the late 2000s when the value of houses plunged.) Most of the *Forbes 400* started with millions in capital and, however they may have originally acquired it, basically compounded it through investment, often speculative—that is, seeking to make a fast profit buying and selling stocks and bonds (or whole corporations) on a gamble that the stock market would go up or down. Other members of the *Forbes 400* in recent decades have included inheritors like the six heirs of Sam Walton and seven heirs of H. L. Hunt, who have never had to work or take much risk at all as their inherited investment appreciated. (See the *Forbes 400* annual issue to survey how various ones made or augmented their fortunes, and what generalizations can be drawn.) To be sure, "work," "risk," and managerial skill are required in managing investment funds and playing the market—though rich people typically hire professional investment managers, who only earn a small percentage of what the owners do. But isn't there also an **equivocation** here in the definition of these terms from their description of risk and work in putting one's capital into and personally running a company for a long term, to a description of impersonally managing vast capital funds, buying and selling whole companies as an occupation, or making a quick killing on Wall Street, where the risk is essentially that of gambling—not generally regarded as a socially beneficial occupation? Where is the "deferral of gratification"? And how much do these activities contribute to job creation or investment in "research and development and education"? Indeed, one of the most common current liberal lines of argument is that America's economy has stagnated precisely because of the drastic shift in investment from high job-producing industries into financial speculation and profitable, but unproductive and low-employment, industries like gambling casinos and lotteries.

At the other end of the socioeconomic scale, Jonathan Kozol's books *Savage Inequalities* and *The Shame of the Nation* present very concrete descriptions of the squalid conditions of inner-city schools and neighborhoods and their causes in the flight of businesses and middle-class residents to the suburbs, taking with them jobs and local tax revenue needed to fund schools—while tax support for education in general has declined through Reaganomic policy cuts at the federal, state, and local levels. Do you think the *Wall Street Journal*, George Will, or you would be able to make a persuasive case that the problems of these people and the "5 million more people living below the poverty line" since 2006, at the official poverty threshold for one person of $10,294 (Sklar) are attributable primarily to poor individuals' lack of "risk-taking and hard work that allow Americans to climb the income ladder so rapidly" (*Wall Street Journal*, November

13, 2007)? Or that American society "offers upward mobility equally to all who accept its rewarding disciplines" (Will)—to inner-city or rural children the same as to suburban children of billionaires, who tend to go to the most expensive private schools and colleges?

You can see, then, how conservatives attempt to set the agenda of public awareness on these issues by propagating the abstract case that allowing the rich to get richer will ultimately help everyone else more than would raising taxes and other restrictions on the rich in order to directly provide better education and jobs for the poor and middle class, as liberals argue in the concrete terms of Sklar and Kozol. So a more advanced conservative case would need to refute liberals' concrete evidence rather than evading it through abstractions, and in your further study you should see if you can find such advanced conservative arguments. For example, conservative think tanks like the Heritage Foundation produce statistically based reports on poverty and income mobility contradicting liberals' data, and these conservative studies prompt counter-rebuttals from liberal economists and journalists, in an unending process of give-and-take.

ANALYZING STATISTICAL TRICKS

The following is based on a student paper pursuing these and related issues.

> Conservative rhetoric on Reaganomics plays heavily on "**plain folks** appeals" attempting to persuade us that trickle-down economics have benefited the middle class and poor at least as much as the rich, and on **appeals to pity** for the virtuous rich, who are unfairly punished by high taxes and excess government regulation, to the detriment of all of us. So conservatives argue that there is no solid proof that Reaganomics policies created a large income disparity gap. In an article for the *Weekly Standard* (July 1, 1996, 19), "Wealth Gap Claptrap," John Weicher, senior fellow at the Hudson Institute and chief economist at the Office of Management and Budget during the Reagan administration, uses Federal Reserve Board statistics to show that "The total wealth of American households increased by over $4 trillion between 1983 and 1992.... Average wealth per household increased by about 11 percent." He claims that the liberal rhetoric just pushes the wealth gap myth in order to gain support for unneeded increased taxes, government spending,

and regulation. He ends his argument, "Yes, the rich are getting richer. And the poor are getting richer. And they're doing it more or less equally."

A careful reading reveals several possible fallacies in Weicher's claim that all classes have gotten wealthier at about an equal rate. Let's say a family in the middle class, with net worth of $100,000, a family with $10 million, and a billionaire all gained 11% over a decade. That means a gain of $11,000 for the first family (about $1,100 per year), but $1.10 million for the second, and $110 million for the third. Did all gain equally, in terms of purchasing power rather than percentage points? In addition, one of the things that those of us in the middle class, who are unable to save or invest much at all, have a hard time understanding about wealth is that rich people aren't just rich, but they are highly likely to keep getting richer all the time, because most of their money is in investments that normally appreciate and compound every year, so every million dollars compounding at, say 10% a year, will be worth over two million in ten years.

In several of his books and articles, liberal economist and *New York Times* columnist Paul Krugman provides further refutation of arguments like Weicher's that downplay the growing gap in income and wealth since the eighties. Krugman points out the difference between *total* or *average* (Weicher's terms) and *median*. Total income or wealth is calculated by adding up all the family incomes or net worths, and their average calculated by dividing the total by the number of families. (If you total or average Bill Gates's wealth and that of a homeless street person, it would look like the latter is a billionaire.) Median income or wealth, a much more meaningful measure, is the one at the middle, in the sense that there are the same number of families above and below it. Krugman has similar figures as Weicher's, that from 1979 to 1989 average family income rose 11 percent, but asserts, "70% of the rise in average family income went to the top 1%," while "the median family income rose only 4 percent" (137–138). In a later article, Krugman adds, "In 1998 the top 1 percent started at $230,000. In turn, 60 percent of the gains of that top 1 percent went to the top 0.1 percent, those with incomes of more than $790,000. And almost half of those gains went to a mere 13,000 taxpayers, the top 0.01 percent, who had an income of at least $3.6 million and an average income of $17 million" ("For Richer," 65). In light of Krugman's figures, Weicher's claim about the *total* national growth of wealth also means little, because the small percentage at the top accounted for most of the growth, just as it skewed average income and wealth upward, while the bottom 40% have seen their income and wealth go down.

In tax policy, liberals argue for highly progressive rates—which is to say that the percentage rate you are taxed goes up more sharply the more you make, while conservatives favor pretty much the same rate for all income levels, which they say is the most fair policy. The same differences apply in conservatives' call for lowering taxes by the same rate for all classes, versus the call by liberals, most recently President Obama, for lowering taxes for the middle class and poor but raising them on the rich.

Let's oversimplify and round off a bit just to illustrate the general principle. If a middle-class family earning, say, $30,000 a year, had their rate cut by 50%, from something like 26% to 13% (about the current rate), they'd save about $3,900 per year—which is fine with liberals, though their policies would save them more through taxing the rich more. After his first cuts, President George W. Bush appeared on TV with such a family proudly showing a blow-up of a check for their couple of thousand dollars refund. Did they benefit equally with the rich, whose taxes were cut by about the same rate? Well, yes and no.

Consider the example of Bill Gates, whose net worth was about $61 billion in 2012—back up from $50 billion after the 2008 crash—according to *Forbes* magazine's annual list of the 400 richest Americans. Also simplifying to a round number of $60 billion—hey, what's a billion here or there?—and not taking account of adjustments to taxable income like deductions and many other ways rich people can avoid paying much income tax at all, let's modestly estimate an annual return on investments of that much at 10%, or $6 billion in taxable income.

This means the following, in very rough approximations. In 1980, before President Reagan started cutting income tax, the rate for the top bracket was 70% on income over about $300,000 (though brackets have always been staggered so the rate is lower on the portion of income below that level). The 1980 tax on $6 billion income @ 70% = $4.2 billion, leaving $1.8 billion in income after taxes (without any dent in the original net worth). The 2007 tax on $6 billion income @ 35% = $2.1 billion, leaving $3.9 billion income after taxes—a saving of some $2.1 billion for one family for one year. So at the same percentage-rate cut, one family would save $3,900 and the other $2.1 billion.

Both benefited equally, right? After President Bush lowered rates again for all classes, did he ask Gates to appear with him showing his refund check?

Next, just for fun, let's extend this hypothetical analysis to a flat tax system like that proposed by Steve Forbes. At the same rate on all brackets, like 12%, the above family earning $30,000 would have owed $4,200 less than at their 1980 rate of 28%, leaving them $22,500 after taxes—a reduction of $4,200. If Bill Gates's income is $6 billion, though, he would now pay only $720 million—$3.48 billion less than at the 1980 rate and $1.38 billion less than at the current rate! (Considering that Steve Forbes happens to be the publisher of *Forbes* magazine, as well as a regular among its 400 richest Americans, might his flat tax proposal have been a case of special pleading?) So the catch in flat-rate proposals is that they predictably will vastly benefit the rich over any progressive tax.

Columnist Holly Sklar writes, "Tax cuts will save the top 1 percent a projected $715 billion between 2001 and 2010. And cost us $715 billion in mounting national debt plus interest." Of course, the rich repay some of what they get back from tax cuts in additional taxes on their increased earnings, providing jobs, etc. However, defenders of supply-side economics would need to prove that these additional revenues exceed what the rich would have paid at a higher rate—sort of a hard sell in light of the record government deficits under both presidents Reagan and George W. Bush.

The trouble with most of us mere middle-class mortals is that we just can't wrap our minds around the meaning of wealth at that stratospheric level, so we project our own psychology to that level—a state of mind that conservative propagandists exploit with their appeals to fear of tax increases. In class discussion about this, when we heard that the top tax rate before 1980 was 70%, some students got indignant and argued that this rate was totally unfair. I think this was because they were imagining how that percentage would deprive them or their families of subsistence income. Conservative talking heads play on this middle-class mentality by charging that a rate like 70% is "confiscatory"—as though the government, as under Communism, is taking away 70% of everything a family owns. This thinking shows lack of imagination in several ways. First, because most of our families don't have much net worth beyond a mortgaged house and a financed car, we do not understand that the income taxes paid by the very rich do not cut into their total wealth at all. They do not in fact owe any income tax on that net worth or on annual compounding of it, even amounting to billions, that is plowed back into the principal, until and unless they sell off some profits (in which case they only have to pay a 15% capital gains tax); they just pay property taxes on business and residential property. So their income tax is based only on their actual income for the year, which usually is a small, easily affordable amount *relative to their net worth*. In fact, rich people often have their accountants arrange things so they report little or no yearly income, just to avoid paying taxes. In conclusion, the harshness of taxes should not be judged by how much we have to pay, but on how much we have left after taxes, both in income and net worth. In a class discussion, I asked my classmates, "Would you rather earn $30,000, pay only $3,900 tax on it at 13%, and have $26,100 left; or earn $6 billion, pay a "confiscatory" $4.2 billion in taxes at 70%—and have $1.8 billion left for the year, compounding a $60 billion net worth?" There were no takers for the lower tax rate.

Another area where our middle-class imaginations are limited is understanding what the super-rich do with their surplus money. We're inclined to think in terms of just spending it all on personal luxuries and going on sprees. But most people at the multimillion-dollar level can't begin to spend all their money (they are pretty foolish if they do). The first thing most do, as noted earlier, is re-invest their surplus to keep compounding their net worth and corporate ownership, widening the gap between them and everyone else. Even more important are all the forms of *power* that money can buy—running for office; gaining governmental favoritism through campaign contributions to politicians and parties; hiring lobbying, public relations, and law firms; monopolizing ownership of corporations and media; being able to set prices and wages to their advantage; etc., etc. Maybe their most effective exercise of power is to hire publicists and control the media to persuade all of us peasants how wonderful the rich are and why they deserve ever-lower taxes and less government regulation. I have not been able to find any conservative sources that have a real rebuttal to this line of argument about the power that money can buy, the strongest one in support of the case that there has been a scarily increasing gap of wealth and power in America.

SUMMARY OF SUSPICIOUS STATISTICAL ARGUMENTS

In conclusion, we always need to keep in mind the implications of economic statistics for each individual, not just abstract social aggregates, and to be on guard against arguments that overwhelm us with compilations of statistics that may look impressive but that obscure individual realities. The following is a summary of some patterns of rhetorically suspicious statistical arguments of the kind we have surveyed here.

1. Arguments that play up the large amount of taxes paid by the wealthy (and the relatively small amount paid by the middle class or poor) in a single year, or a growing amount over a period of years, without also comparing actual dollar income and net worth among the classes being compared.
2. Arguments that play up a total or average (as opposed to median) increase in income or net worth in the entire society or within one broad bracket, without factoring in large increases at the very top of the society or bracket that might skew upward the total or average, and that consequently downplay relative losses for those in the middle and lower sectors. Similarly, arguments that play up the total amount spent by government in a field like education without factoring in large discrepancies in spending between wealthy and poor sectors.
3. Arguments that play up the same percentage change in different brackets of income, net worth, or tax reductions as alleged evidence of equitable results in all groups, while downplaying the large differences in dollar amounts among the groups resulting from an equal percentage change in each.
4. Arguments that play up the benefits of one part of a policy change (e.g., reduction of income taxes) while downplaying the negative effects of another part of that change (e.g., increase in Social Security or other taxes); or conversely, arguments that play up the negative effects (e.g., more people becoming wealthy at other classes' expense under Reaganomics) while downplaying, as conservatives say liberals do, the positive effects (closing of prior loopholes, resulting in more tax revenue).

AN OUTLINE OF CONSERVATIVE AND LIBERAL OR LEFTIST ARGUMENTS ON THE RICH, THE POOR, AND THE MIDDLE CLASS

The following is an outline of the broad points of opposition between conservatives and liberals or leftists on the topics in this chapter. On some of these points, liberals and leftists agree; on others, differences between them are indicated. In keeping with good semantic principles, the outline is meant to be open-ended. The facts that the liberal/leftist arguments get the last word here and are more numerous should simply serve as a challenge to you and your classmates to use this as a point of departure, seeing what effective conservative rebuttals you can find. So "the last word" in this outline, this chapter, and this book is, "etc., etc., etc."

The Conservative Position

The basic position of President Reagan, both Presidents Bush, and their conservative supporters is that American government has been overloaded trying to provide for the public welfare in programs like education, Social Security, Medicare, welfare, unemployment insurance, minimum wage laws, and so on. Moreover, excessive taxation and bureaucratic government regulation of business (especially for environmental protection) have stifled the productive power of free enterprise. This overload on government has led to inflation, deficit spending, and dependency of beneficiaries of programs like welfare on "handouts." Therefore, if government spending on domestic programs is reduced and taxes cut by equal percentage rates across all income lines (with the largest savings going to wealthy individuals and corporations), private enterprise will be freed to function more effectively; it will be more efficient than government and the public sector of the economy in generating jobs, producing more tax revenue, and filling other public needs. The reason these beneficial "Reaganomic" policies haven't been fully effective is that they haven't been given an adequate chance to work, their full implementation having been blocked by Democrats in Congress and other leftist bureaucrats and special interest groups purely because of their partisan and selfish motives. Deficit spending has increased only because Democrats in Congress rejected every effort by President Reagan and both Presidents Bush to reduce the budget.

Conservatives also argue that

1. Budget and tax cuts in the federal government under Reagan and both Bushes, and in states like California since Proposition 13 in 1978, which capped property tax rates for businesses as well as homeowners, have just trimmed the fat, eliminating unnecessary programs and administrative waste and leaving intact essential programs and the "safety net" of support for the truly needy.
2. Flat-rate taxes and tax cuts are fairer than progressive taxes because all income levels pay and benefit from cuts at the same rate.
3. Government spending in many areas such as education and welfare can be more properly and efficiently handled by states and localities than by the federal government; the funding burden should be shifted to them.
4. Much of the overload on government has resulted from selfish, excessive demands for "entitlements" from special interests like welfare recipients, minorities, the elderly, veterans, teachers, and students. These groups have become dependent on handouts and have lost their incentive to work.
5. Individual initiative, not government programs, is the best solution to social problems. Conservatives believe in equality of opportunity, not an inaccessible equality of outcome as liberals do, and believe that all Americans *do* have equal opportunity to succeed. Everyone who tries hard enough can get a good job and be financially successful. It is usually a person's own fault if he or she is poor or unemployed. The poor should just try harder and be more virtuous.
6. Spending on national defense is an exception to the need to cut government because increases in the eighties were necessary to defeat Russia in the arms race (Communism's collapse vindicated Reagan's hard-line policies); a strong defense is still necessary because of terrorism and other potential threats, like Saddam Hussein and the Taliban in 2001, or Iran more recently, to American security.
7. The most effective way to reduce poverty and unemployment is to permit the rich to get richer—the trickle-down theory or supply-side economics—because their increased spending trickles down to benefit all other segments of society proportionately. The concentration of wealth at the top is not a zero-sum game, in which the gains of the rich come at the expense of the middle class or poor.

8. Wealthy individuals and corporate executives can be trusted to use their increased benefits for the public welfare because in order to attain and maintain their position they have to be exceptionally intelligent, hardworking, honest, and civic-minded.
9. Most rich people have worked hard for their money and have risked their investments, so they shouldn't be penalized by high taxes and government regulations that stifle their incentive to work and to invest. Executives' high salaries are proportionate to the profits they have produced for their companies.
10. Minimum-wage laws, high corporate or individual taxes, and excessive regulations—especially in environmental, safety, and health issues—force industries to move their operations to lower-cost locations in the United States or to other countries. Such increased expenses are also passed on to consumers in higher prices, so they are self-defeating.
11. The rich are generous in sharing their wealth; the more money they are allowed to keep, the more they give to charities.
12. Wealth is compatible with religious, and especially Christian, morality. Many wealthy people like Nelson Bunker Hunt use their wealth to support religious organizations and causes.
13. Leftist criticisms of Reagan, George W. Bush, and the rich often consist of "sour grapes" rationalizations by government bureaucrats, intellectuals, teachers, journalists, or public employees who are just unwilling or unable to make it themselves in the private sector and who are jealous of those who do. These "bleeding hearts" sentimentalize the poor.
14. Leftist teachers' and other public employees' arguments may reflect ethnocentric bias, conflict of interest, or special pleading, since members of these groups benefit personally from higher taxation and the resulting increases in government spending. Likewise, arguments by leftist intellectuals may be self-interested, concealing their drive to replace the rich as the new ruling class.
15. History has shown that, in spite of all its faults, capitalism or free enterprise is a more efficient and humane economic system than any form of socialism or mixed economy.
16. Statistically based arguments: Empirical evidence that Reaganomics worked includes the facts that the 1980s saw a reduction in inflation and the longest period of steady growth in the American economy since World War II; millions of new jobs were created; the rich paid higher dollar amounts and an increased percentage of tax revenues, and total tax revenues

increased. Liberal-leftist claims of a growing gap between the rich and the middle class and poor are based on faulty statistical analyses. There has been much more socioeconomic mobility in recent decades than liberals want to admit, with many people moving out of poverty into the middle class, and many others dropping out of the upper income brackets.

The Liberal and Leftist Positions

Democracy in America is being destroyed and replaced by plutocracy—rule by and for the rich. Reagan and both Bushes have been agents of plutocratic special interests, as are most Republican and Democratic politicians, including President Kennedy, Clinton, and Obama. These politicians appeal to liberal constituencies to get elected but then sell them out on many if not most issues. Reaganomic policies have had the effect, intentionally or unintentionally, of entrenching plutocracy by making the rich richer and the middle class and the poor poorer and by eliminating needed welfare programs and productive areas of public spending and employment. Government spending primes the pump when the economy slumps and provides services not offered by the private sector, while progressive taxation serves to reduce the gap of wealth and power between the rich and the rest of the population. (This describes Keynesian economics, favored by liberals, but leftists believe that Keynesian policies are designed ultimately to try to save capitalism from its fatal flaws, which will nevertheless eventually lead to its collapse and replacement by a fully socialistic economy.) The conservative line of argument against both Keynesian and socialistic economics is largely a propaganda program engineered by wealthy special interests to rationalize their own greed. In fact, Reagan and both Bushes consistently proposed budgets that were higher (mainly because of defense increases) than those passed by Congress, but their budget increases amounted to "Keynesian" socialism for the rich, free enterprise for the poor.

Liberals or leftists also make the following arguments. The numbers in parentheses refer to refuted conservative arguments.

1. American cultural conditioning favors the rich by fostering common blocks to clear thinking like authoritarian awe and sentimentality toward the rich, the ethnocentrism and wishful thinking of middle-class people hoping to become rich, and favorable stereotypes of the rich and prejudiced ones of the working class and poor.

2. (9) There is often little correlation between how hard people work or how much risk they take and how much money they make. Many of those who make the most money don't make it through work at all but through investments (often inherited) and speculation, while many of those who work the hardest and at the greatest risk (e.g., farmworkers, coal miners, police, firefighters) make the least. Corporate executive salaries have gotten totally out of proportion to performance—in many cases, CEOs have received vastly increased income even when their companies have lost money—partly because of conflicts of interest between CEOs and boards of directors who determine their compensation.
3. (5) Conservative "try harder" arguments fail to recognize the basic inequities structured into a capitalist economy and the external economic forces—national and worldwide economic trends, inflation, recession, discrepancies in opportunity between different geographical areas or demographic groups, and so on—that often make individual effort futile. In a free-enterprise economy, there is no certainty of full employment, of a job being available for everyone who needs one, or of a minimum wage above poverty level. Conservatives have constructed a straw-man leftist who demands nothing less than total equality of outcome from social policies, but most liberals and leftists simply believe that present-day America is far from presenting equal opportunity for all, so that their policies are only aimed at bringing about that *opportunity*.
4. (7) There is no conclusive evidence that the trickle-down theory has ever worked in practice or ever will. Contrary to conservative claims that supply-side tax cuts would actually increase tax revenues, federal and local revenues have been lower than they would have been under previous progressive rates, and huge deficits have resulted at both the national and local levels. Much of what the rich get back in tax cuts is often invested not in job-producing enterprises but in personal luxuries, tax dodges, hedges against inflation, speculation, corporate takeovers resulting in monopoly and inflated prices for consumers and lost jobs for workers, or investments in foreign countries that exploit cheap labor there while taking jobs and money out of the United States.
5. (7, 8, 10) Outlandish corporate profits and gaps between executives and employees in recent decades belie conservatives' claims that the rich getting richer benefits everyone, as well

as their appeals to pity for overtaxed, overregulated corporations. Businesses often use these appeals to pity and the appeal to fear of their relocating within the United States or abroad as blackmail to get their way. Globalization and outsourcing of jobs simply exploit the absence in poorer countries of minimum-wage laws, labor unions, and environmental, safety, and health regulations. Corporate relocation abroad, motivated by greed, has devastated American workers and contradicts conservative claims that capitalists are virtuous and patriotic.

6. While much money spent in the private sector does not trickle down to the rest of society, virtually all money spent in the public sector "trickles up" back into the private sector. Spending on education, public health, welfare, and so on is a good investment by society that pays off in higher productivity. Spending by tax-funded public agencies (e.g., universities) creates jobs and subsidizes private-sector contractors for construction, equipment, and services. Corporate interests want (and depend on) these subsidies without wanting to pay the taxes needed to fund them.

7. The private sector is just as wasteful and inefficient as the public sector, and the most waste in both occurs at the executive levels, where spending is administered (primarily in administrators' own interests). Thus budget cuts resulting from laws like Proposition 13 in California have left governmental administrative "fat" intact while bankrupting local governments, causing layoffs of rank-and-file public employees and harmful cuts in essential services like education and law enforcement. The conservative belief that there is a vast amount of fat that can be trimmed from government agencies at the rank-and-file level is often just wishful thinking or rationalization of conservatives' politically motivated desire to squeeze out liberal constituencies served by government spending.

8. (3) As a result of local tax cuts like Proposition 13, state and local governments are even more hard-pressed financially than the federal government, so conservative claims that funding responsibilities are better handled at the local level are simply rationalizations or passing the buck.

9. (9) Those who can afford to pay the most taxes and who benefit most from a prosperous society—that is, the rich—should be expected to pay the most. Flat-rate tax cuts disproportionately benefit the rich and widen the gap in wealth and ownership of income-producing holdings like stocks, bonds, real estate,

and farms, enabling the rich to increase their power in all of the following ways.

10. The rich can buy political influence with both the Republican and Democratic parties and government officials, causing legislation to be passed in their interest and against that of the middle class and poor, particularly in tax policies, such as regressive cuts in income, corporation, inheritance, and property taxes that in recent decades have sharply reduced the burden on the rich.
11. As a result of 10, the tax burden has shifted increasingly from the rich to the middle class, especially in tax increases for Social Security and Medicare and, at the local and state levels, in sales taxes. As a further result, members of the overtaxed middle class vote to support cuts in public services that harm themselves and society as a whole but not the rich, who don't depend on these services, such as public education, Social Security, public health insurance, welfare, law enforcement, public libraries, and public transportation. Middle class people rationalize these cuts by turning the poor, "big government," and public employees into scapegoats, blaming them instead of the rich for the financial squeeze on themselves.
12. The rich can use the power of hiring and firing to force workers and students (as future workers) into compliance with pro-rich attitudes; because we have to cater to them to get or keep a job, we tend to fall into doublethink compartmentalized thinking to rationalize our servitude to them.
13. The rich are able to create a favorable public image of themselves through ownership or sponsorship of news and entertainment media, advertising, and public relations. They exert a large degree of control over education as donors or university trustees and by sponsoring research in both universities and private think tanks that supports their interests.
14. (8) Many rich people and corporations get away with criminal or unethical activity that causes relatively little public indignation or opposition from law enforcement agencies, compared to actions by lower-class criminals or "leeches." The middle class tends to have a double standard or **selective vision** in playing down misconduct by the rich and playing up that by the poor. How can we expect poor people to respect the law or act morally when those at the top of society set such a poor example?
15. It is often affluent conservative businesspeople who benefit most from the government subsidies that conservatives claim

they oppose (compartmentalized thinking): subsidies to farmers (including for food stamps); to insurance companies, doctors, pharmaceutical manufacturers, and sellers of health insurance; to bankers for student loans; to bondholders for government debts, and so on.

16. (6) Wealthy people and corporations control the defense industry, which receives the biggest government subsidy of all and whose only customer is the government. Spending on weapons that are only intended to be destroyed or replaced by more advanced ones is disastrous for the national economy. (But the defense industry is exempt from conservative attacks on government bureaucracy and waste, because it produces big corporate profits and campaign contributions.) More and more of our national income has been eaten up by this wasteful spending, which is a major cause of inflation and deficit spending and which has squeezed out spending on more productive domestic programs like education and employment for public works. During the Cold War, the military-industrial complex and its wealthy executives became the tail that wagged the dog of defense policy in their own self-interest, artificially perpetuating tensions with Russia to bolster their profits and power (mirroring the military establishment in Russia that was similarly self-interested). The main reason Communism collapsed was not the American arms buildup but the inept, dictatorial bureaucrats who were running the Soviet Union's government and economy. But because American conservatives are always partial to militarism, they tend to be blind to the military as a special interest and to fraud and waste in military spending, which has accelerated again after September 11 and the Iraq war, rationalized by appeals to fear of terrorism.

17. The rich can influence foreign policy to protect their foreign investments, markets, and sources of natural resources and cheap labor. International competition for markets has frequently been the cause of wars throughout history.

18. The wealthy profit from wars that are conducted in their class interests and that consume weapons that they produce, but they and their children rarely risk their own lives fighting in those wars. Any business interest that profits from a war should be expected to pay increased taxes to finance it.

19. (11) Rich people on the whole do not give a great amount to charity, relative to their income or net worth, and they benefit

from what they give through tax deductions, trusteeships, and a favorable public image as philanthropists or supporters of religion.

20. (12) Attempts to reconcile wealth with Christianity amount to hypocritical rationalizations, since they are completely contrary to the teachings of Jesus Christ.

21. (15) Some semisocialist countries (e.g., Denmark, Sweden) have surpassed America in per capita income, quality of life, and well-functioning democracy, while some capitalist countries (e.g., Saudi Arabia, South Africa under apartheid, Chile under Pinochet, El Salvador under Duarte, the Philippines under Marcos) are plutocratic, right-wing dictatorships, and Americans' prosperity and freedom are paid for at the expense of poor people in those countries, which are in effect colonies of American corporations.

22. (16) Statistically based arguments: Since the 1980s, the income of the richest 1 percent of Americans has skyrocketed, and the gap between the rich, middle class, and poor has become greater than at any time since the 1920s. The rich obviously are paying more in taxes because their *income* is greater in relation to everyone else's, thanks largely to Reaganomic subsidies, and their after-tax savings have increasingly outstripped everyone else's. Inflation has been reduced mainly through reduction of real income for the majority of workers, largely through outsourcing of jobs to Third World sweatshops. Economic growth since the eighties has been slower than in previous decades, and the jobs created have been mostly low-wage ones. The main reason more people are working is that two or more people in the same household have been forced to work in order to make the real income previously earned by one; most Americans now have to work more hours to make the same real income they did thirty years ago.

Topics for Discussion and Writing

1. A rebuttal to earlier versions of Sklar's arguments cited here can be found in "Why Try Holly Sklar's Socialist Plans for Economy When United States Is Doing Just Fine?" by Elizabeth Carnell, posted on LeftWatch.com, September 1, 1999 (www.leftwatch.com/holly_sklar/sklar001.html). Carnell argues that "the truth is Americans are much better off today than they were even 20 years ago, and the

United States still enjoys the highest standard of living in the world." Consider whether Carnell might be committing a version of #2 in "Suspicious Statistical Arguments" in the above list—that is, are all, or even most, Americans better off and enjoying the highest standard of living? Is the "average American"? The "median-income American?" (She provides no supporting data here. You might check her data with the Bureau of Labor Statistics studies cited by Sklar for "the average worker.") Look up Carnell's article or her more recent ones to see how fully it refutes Sklar on other points.
2. Find some current versions of economic arguments between liberals and conservatives like those cited in this chapter, and apply this kind of rhetorical and statistical analysis to evaluating them.
3. Since around 2009 when gas prices escalated, along with record-setting oil company profits and executive income, the American Petroleum Institute, the industry trade association or lobby, has sponsored a widespread campaign of television and print ads under the signature of EnergyTomorrow.org. The ads played up the industry's investment in developing alternative sources of energy, along with strong "plain folks" appeal; they are signed, "THE *PEOPLE* OF AMERICA'S OIL AND NATURAL GAS INDUSTRY." (Do you suppose "the people" commissioned or wrote these ads?) One shows a photo of a young, obviously middle-class couple with two children in their modest breakfast room, over the headline, "Do you own an oil company?" Another shows a pie chart indicating that only 1.5% of stock shareholders belong to "corporate management," while "the majority of oil and natural gas company shareholders are middle-class U.S. households with mutual fund investments, pension accounts or other retirement accounts and mutual fund investments." The conclusion is, "So when Congress starts talking about raising energy taxes or taking 'excess profits' from U.S. oil companies, look at the facts and ask yourself, 'who does that really hurt?'" How might their breakdown of stock ownership be a **half-truth** in terms of what amount of stock is actually owned by the different categories collectively and individuals within them? And how would this reflect on who would be most hurt by raising taxes on oil company profits, along the lines of the analysis of the effects of tax increases and cuts in this chapter? See if you find the answers at the EnergyTomorrow.org website or elsewhere.
4. In his *New York Times* column (July 1, 2008), David Brooks wrote, "When he is swept up in rhetorical fervor, Obama occasionally says that his campaign is 90 percent funded by small donors. He has indeed had great success with small donors, but only about 45 percent

of his money comes from donations of $200 or less." How might this argument by Obama be similarly fallacious to the API ads in #2?
5. Use "An Outline of Conservative and Liberal or Leftist Arguments on the Rich, the Poor, and the Middle Class" as a point of departure for individual or group study toward a research paper, looking for conservative rebuttals of the liberal and leftist lines of argument.

Appendix
Glossary of Logical and Rhetorical Fallacies

Sometimes after students have started to study fallacies, they are inclined to approach arguments searching just for fallacies in them, only looking for points to pick apart, rather than also looking for good, fallacy-free arguments or those that effectively point out fallacies in someone else's argument. The latter approach should be part of your goal in studying this list of logical and rhetorical fallacies. ("Logical fallacies" is the usual term, referring mainly to unintentional flaws in reasoning. "Rhetorical fallacies" here refers to more devious motives in, and modes of, argument.)

Students sometimes also fret excessively over what is the proper label for a fallacious argument, rather than simply explaining in their own words how the argument is fallacious; pinning the label to the fallacy may be worthwhile, but it is secondary to showing your understanding of the argument's substantive flaws. Another source for fretting is which of several similar terms is the "correct" one; several of these terms, however, are synonymous or closely enough related so that they may be interchangeable. Here are some clusters of related fallacies, gathered from the following alphabetical glossary.

- Presenting only one side of a story, or slanting an account to one side: propaganda, special pleading, stacking the deck, half-truth, double standard, selective vision, cleans and dirties, tu quoque (in the sense of someone pointing out legitimately the fallacy in opponents who are guilty of the same fault of which they accuse others).
- Oversimplification: overgeneralization, sweeping generalization, either-or thinking, false dilemma, false dichotomy, reductive fallacy, not accounting for all factors or variables.
- Hasty conclusion or non sequitur: inadequate evidence, unrepresentative sample, argument from the exception.
- Inconsistency: compartmentalized thinking, self-contradiction, doublethink, shifting ground, equivocation, "I Won't, but I Will," "Heads I Win, Tails You Lose."
- Distraction: begging the question, evading the issue, shifting ground, red herring, irrelevance.
- Personal attacks: ad hominem, name-calling, straw man, poisoning the well, smearing, character assassination, tu quoque, guilt by association, derision, distortion.
- Appeals to widespread opinion or common practice: *ad populum,* bandwagon, plain folks, appeal to the past or resistance to change, common practice, two wrongs make a right.
- Emotional appeal: appeals to pity or fear, demagogy, scare tactics, sentimentality, religiosity, flag-waving, jingoism.

GLOSSARY OF LOGICAL AND RHETORICAL FALLACIES

ad hominem. Latin for argument "against the man." The rhetorical fallacy of attacking the character or motives of an opponent as a means of discrediting or evading the substance of his or her arguments. Variants include **name-calling**, poisoning the well, smearing, and character assassination.

ad populum. Latin, appeal "to the people." The logical fallacy of arguing that something is true because many or most people believe it is, or that a policy is valid because many or most agree with it. The fallacy lies in the fact that mass opinion is not always well informed, accurate, or morally just. When *is* it valid to cite majority opinion in the general population, or within any particular group, to support your position? When you can present evidence that the majority is well informed and has benefited from the policy you advocate.

appeal to authority or **transfer of authority**. This logical fallacy takes three common forms. One is citing as a source on a particular subject someone who is an authority on *some* subject but not the one at issue, or even someone who is only, in Daniel Boorstin's phrase, "well-known for being well-known." (The celebrity endorsement ad is the most frequent occasion for this form.) Another form is citing the opinion of a source who is an authority on the issue as sufficient in itself, without presenting the evidence on which that opinion is based. The opinions of those who are authorities on a subject are likely to be supported with better evidence than those of nonexperts, but their evidence still needs to be documented. The third form is when a genuine authority is cited, but the authority's opinion diverges from the opinions of other authorities or is otherwise suspect. This might happen when the cited authority has a conflict of interest or holds an opinion about an issue that differs from the consensus of other authorities in a field. To avoid this third form of the fallacy, you should acknowledge the difference and present a case for why this authority's word should prevail over others' if you think it should.

appeal to fear or **scare tactics**. Along with its flip side, **appeal to pity**, the most common form of emotional appeal—most prominently in calls for war or, more recently, protection against terrorism. This is another case where a judgment call is always necessary to determine whether such an appeal has legitimate grounds, when it is a perfectly valid line of argument, or whether it is deliberately fabricated or exaggerated to frighten people into compliance with those in power, or to attract a profitable media audience.

appeal to the past or tradition, or **resistance to change**. The logical fallacy of arguing for a policy only because it has been followed in the past or is a tradition in one's culture, regardless of whether it might be outdated.

appeal to pity. A common variety of **sentimentality**. The judgment call here is whether the people being defended truly deserve pity or whether the audience's heartstrings are being tugged on fraudulently. For example, in law courts, attorneys will often attempt to elicit the jury's pity for their clients to help the clients' case. But pitying someone is not a good justification for thinking that he or she did or did not commit a crime or that his or her legal claims have any warrant. Evidence is needed for that.

argument from the converse. The logical fallacy of starting with a statement whose truth has been established, in the form of "All (or most) Xs are Y," then jumping to the converse conclusion, "All (or most) Ys are X," which is a form of **non sequitur**. This fallacy can usually be explained in terms of logical classes and subclasses or sets and subsets, as in mathematics, and illustrated through circle diagrams, as in figure 2.1, which indicates that all communists and Communists are socialists but not all socialists are communists or Communists.

argument from the exception. The logical fallacy of supporting an argument with a case that is an exception to the rule, contrary to the larger body of evidence supporting the opposing side; synonymous with an unrepresentative sample.

bandwagon. A variety of *ad populum*, attempting to lure you to get on the bandwagon, to agree with a policy or take an action because "everybody's doing it." Extremely common in advertising.

begging the question. A fallacy in deductive logic in which a conclusion depends on prior acceptance of a premise whose truth has not been established or is disputable. Often used synonymously with **circular argument**. In common usage, "begs the question" is often used synonymously, but erroneously, with "raises the question" rather than its accurate meaning of "evades the issue."

changing the subject or **shifting ground**. This rhetorical fallacy occurs when people have no effective response to a refutation of an argument they have made, so they bring up a different line of argument on the same subject while hoping no one notices that they are evading the issue.

circular argument. A logical fallacy in which a reason given in support of a conclusion presupposes the truth of the conclusion, or in which the conclusion depends on prior acceptance of a premise that is believed only because the conclusion is already believed. "I believe the president is telling the truth." "How do you know that?" "Because he's a God-fearing man." "How do you know that?" "Because he says so." Another form is the attempt to support a premise with words that simply repeat the premise in slightly different language; for example, "Capitalism is desirable because it promotes free enterprise." Free enterprise is just another name for capitalism, so the argument does not give a reason why capitalism, or free enterprise, is desirable.

cleans and dirties. The rhetorical fallacy of using connotatively loaded language applying all positive words to your side and all negative ones to your opponents', purely for emotional appeal, without sufficient evidence that the words are accurate. Using loaded language like this is not fallacious, however, if it *is* supported by evidence.

common practice. The rhetorical fallacy of justifying a shady ethical practice because "everybody does it." Also see **tu quoque** and **two wrongs make a right**.

compartmentalization or **compartmentalized thinking**. Logical self-contradiction or inconsistency. In its extreme form it results in Orwellian **doublethink**. The concept can also apply to saying one thing but doing another.

demagogy or **demagoguery**. The use of emotional appeal by unscrupulous politicians or other public figures—**demagogues**—to manipulate the ethnocentric beliefs or prejudices of a mass audience for their own benefit.

derision. A form of **ad hominem** in which the opponent's ideas or character are just ridiculed or sneered at without any substantive refutation.

distortion. The rhetorical fallacy of misrepresenting an opponent's ideas, whether unintentionally or intentionally. Related to **straw man**.

double standard. The rhetorical fallacy, or mode of deception, in which a variety of critical standards are applied to opponents but are not applied consistently, not applied as strongly, or not applied at all to one's own views or to the views of people on one's side. See "A Semantic Calculator for Bias in Rhetoric" in Chapter 1, as well as **selective vision** and **stacking the deck**.

doublethink. Coined by George Orwell in his novel *1984* to describe the logical or rhetorical fallacy of being brainwashed by propaganda to believe self-contradictory ideas like "war is peace," "slavery is freedom," "ignorance is strength." Also applicable to abrupt reversals or deceptions in political policies without recognition of an inconsistency. In *1984,* a government reduction in the chocolate ration is announced as an increase, but the people join a mass celebration in gratitude.

either-or. Also known as *false dilemma* or *false dichotomy*. The fallacy of setting two positions in opposition to each other when they might be mutually compatible, or of suggesting that there are only two feasible alternatives when there are in fact others.

emotional appeal. The rhetorical fallacy of invalid appeal to the audience's emotions at the expense of reason. Appeals to emotion are fallacious generally when they appeal to feeling about some truth *as evidence* for it. For example, fearing that global warming is now happening cannot serve as evidence that it is happening. However, if there is firm evidence that global warming really is happening, our fear of the consequences can be used as a good reason supporting a call to action.

equal and opposite extreme. The logical fallacy of rejecting an irrational, extreme position, but then failing to draw the line in lurching to an opposite extreme that is equally irrational, as in critics of the prejudices in white- or male-dominated culture who end up proclaiming the innate superiority of blacks or women, in "reverse racism" or "reverse sexism."

equivocation. The rhetorical fallacy of changing the sense in which a word is used, in the middle of an argument, or of using a definition of it that is not applicable in the context. A mode of **shifting ground**. For example, when people defending capital punishment because they believe it deters potential murderers are confronted with empirical evidence to the contrary, they sometimes respond, "Well, it deters the executed criminal from killing again."

evading the issue. There are several fallacious means of trying to squirm out of acknowledging that one's opponent has made a point that one cannot logically refute, including **begging the question**, **changing the subject**, introducing a **red herring**, **shifting ground**, **ad hominem**, **name-calling**, and **tu quoque** attacks on the opponent.

false analogy or **false equation**. The logical fallacy of arguing that two situations are similar to one another or exactly the same, so that what we accept as true about one should also be accepted about the other, when there are significant differences between them.

faulty causation. Common fallacies in assertions of causes. *Post hoc, ergo propter hoc*: After, therefore because of; assuming (without adequate evidence) that because one thing happened after another one, the first caused the second, or some other confusion of correlation with causation. *Reductive fallacy*: Reducing a probable multiplicity of causes to a single one. *Slippery slope*: Arguing (without adequate evidence) that one action or policy will lead to a whole series of increasingly dire consequences. *Confusion of cause and effect*: Viewing an action or policy as the cause of a particular effect when it might be the effect of a different cause. *Too much or too little?*: Has a policy been unsuccessful because it has been pushed too far or not far enough? *Giving your side credit for positive results*: Along with giving your side credit, you may be blaming the other side for negative results (without adequate evidence). *Blaming the victim*: Placing the blame on the victim of a harmful action or policy rather than on the cause of it.

flag-waving, jingoism. The rhetorical fallacy of emotional appeal deceptively manipulating patriotism and fear of a foreign enemy.

guilt by association. The rhetorical fallacy of smearing opponents by falsely associating them with a disreputable person or organization. It is not fallacious to criticize opponents for their actual, admitted association with disreputable forces.

half-truth. The rhetorical fallacy of **stacking the deck** by playing up only those portions of a truth that favor one's own side, while suppressing mention of other portions that discredit it, as in ads that boast of a certain feature of a brand without mentioning that every other brand of the product has the same feature.

hasty conclusion. The logical fallacy of jumping to a conclusion based on inadequate evidence, an unrepresentative sample, or an **overgeneralization**.

inadequate evidence or **unrepresentative sampling**. In inductive reasoning, the fallacy of drawing a conclusion or making a generalization based on a sampling of evidence, or set of examples, too small to generalize from or unrepresentative of a larger sampling.

inconsistency or **self-contradiction**. The logical fallacy of an argument some of whose parts are inconsistent with, or contradict, others in the same argument or an earlier one by the same author.

inductive leap. A form of **non sequitur** or **hasty conclusion** in which one jumps to an extreme conclusion based on skimpy empirical evidence.

irrelevance. An argument that does not really apply to the point at issue. Whether intentional or unintentional, it is a form of **evading the issue**.

lip service. The rhetorical fallacy of making a public show of belief in a popular cause, such as religion or patriotism, while not practicing what one preaches.

name-calling. The most common variety of **ad hominem**, substituting nasty words describing opponents for reasoned refutation of their arguments. As with other forms of **emotional appeal**, name-calling can be a valid rhetorical method *if you support the name you call someone by sufficient evidence,* or if such evidence has been historically established beyond much dispute—such as, "Hitler, Stalin, and Saddam Hussein were insane, murderous tyrants."

non sequitur. Latin, "it does not follow," that is, one statement does not follow logically from the previous one. The many kinds of non sequitur include deductive arguments in which the conclusion does not follow from the premises, **evading the issue**, **circular argument**, **hasty conclusion**, **inductive leap**, and **faulty causation**. Also a general term for an abrupt change of subject in which the second subject is asserted to be related to the first but isn't.

overgeneralization or **sweeping generalization**. The logical fallacy of making a generalization that is so vague or vast as to be practically useless, or that jumps to a conclusion about a large class of people or things based on an **inadequate** or **unrepresentative sampling**.

oversimplification. The broadest category of the many logical and rhetorical fallacies that reduce a complex set of realities to an overly simplistic, black-and-white explanation.

plain folks. The rhetorical fallacy of a politician or other public figure who in wealth, power, or education is an elitist but who pretends to be a populist, speaking like, and claiming to represent the interests of, the masses of ordinary citizens, often for the purpose of demagogic manipulation.

propaganda. A deliberately one-sided view of any issue, usually produced by governments, political parties and candidates, special interests, and professional agents in their service. Propaganda employs the whole range of rhetorical methods of **stacking the deck**. See Chapter 4.

quotation out of context. The rhetorical fallacy of quoting a few words or sentences from a source text in a manner that makes them appear to have a different meaning than they have within the context of the complete text. This is a common tactic in writers of invective who deliberately distort their opponents' ideas in this manner. It is also used by advertisers of cultural productions to put the most favorable spin on journalistic reviews, as when an ad quotes a review of a movie calling it "spectacular," when the full text reads, "This film is the most spectacular disaster in years."

red herring. The rhetorical fallacy of **changing the subject** by jumping from addressing an issue to dragging in another one, usually strong in **emotional appeal**, to distract attention from the first.

selective vision. The rhetorical fallacy of seeing, or discussing, only your opponents' bad policies and behavior, while turning a blind eye to your own side's similar faults. Synonymous with **double standard**.

sentimentality. The rhetorical fallacy of using excessive or manipulative evocation of positive **emotional appeal**. Words commonly applied to sentimental appeals are "tear-jerking," "corny," and "sappy." Staples of sentimentality are religiosity (a religious posture without any commitment to substantial religious morality), **flag-waving**, images of Mom and apple pie, cute little children and puppy dogs, soap-opera-like **appeal to pity** (as in celebrity journalism's accounts of the tragedies of the rich and famous), and so on. Also used in public relations to fabricate a cosmeticized, saintly image of some public figure or organization. Like other forms of emotional appeal, sentimentality is often employed with **selective vision**, by which one tries to gain sympathy for a favored individual or group while ignoring the fact that an opponent or some other social group might deserve as much or more sympathy. In politics and war, sentimentality is evident in selective emotional appeals for one's own side's causes or forces ("our boys") while the opponents' are demonized.

shifting ground. The logical or rhetorical fallacy of changing your position or line of argument—especially in a contradictory manner—without justification, resulting in **compartmentalized thinking** or **doublethink**. In the 2000 presidential election, when the Florida Supreme Court was overruled by the U.S. Supreme Court to give George W. Bush the victory, Democrats, who usually support the primacy of federal government over state governments, shifted ground in denouncing the U.S. Supreme Court action, while Republicans did the opposite shift.

special pleading. The rhetorical fallacy of claiming to be an objective, neutral analyst in order to conceal the reality that one is an advocate for special interests or one side of an issue, or of arguing that some extenuating circumstances apply—"I'm special"; "This case is special"—when in fact the circumstances are not very special.

stacking the deck. General term for the whole repertory of rhetorical fallacies—including **double standard** and **selective vision**—used to present a **propagandistically** one-sided view, through **playing up**, or "cherry picking," all arguments and evidence in favor of one side while **downplaying** or suppressing altogether all arguments and evidence against that side and in favor of the other side. See "A Semantic Calculator for Bias in Rhetoric" in Chapter 4.

straw man. The rhetorical fallacy of depicting an image of opponents that bears no real resemblance to them or that distorts or oversimplifies their ideas and then claiming that you have disposed of their ideas by refuting the false version of them.

tokenism. A form of **lip service** in which one complies minimally or halfheartedly with a required policy, such as equal-opportunity hiring, with "a token woman" or "a token minority."

tu quoque. Latin, "you too." The rhetorical fallacy of defending your side against an accusation by saying the other side is guilty of the same abuse. A form of **two wrongs make a right**. Tu quoque can be a valid, effective line of argument if it is not used to excuse your side from fault but to point out the other side's hypocrisy in not practicing what they preach to others.

two wrongs make a right. The logical fallacy of rationalizing one's bad behavior on the grounds of **common practice**, **tu quoque**, or "getting even." That is, it's okay for me/us to do this, because you/our opponents have done the same thing. This is frequently practiced with a **double standard**, by which one side—in war, for example—will justify its atrocities or desire to get even, while denying any such justification to the other side.

what do you mean, "we"? The rhetorical fallacy of a falsely all-encompassing "we," as when a teacher says, "We'll have an exam next week," a wealthy government official says, "We all need to make sacrifices in these hard times," a corporate polluter says, "We're all concerned about the environment, or someone who is not in military service and whose life is not at risk says, "We have to go to war."

wishful thinking. The form of rationalization in which people believe what they want to believe, or what benefits them or their allies, rather than drawing reasoned conclusions.

Bibliography

Alterman, Eric. *What Liberal Media? The Truth about Bias and the News.* New York: Basic Books, 2003.

Bagdikian, Ben. *The New Media Monopoly.* Boston: Beacon, 2004.

Barnouw, Eric. *The Sponsor: Notes on a Modern Potentate.* Oxford: Oxford University Press, 1978.

Bleifuss, Joel. "Flack Attack." *In These Times,* September 6, September 20, October 4, 1993.

Bloom, Allan. *The Closing of the American Mind.* New York: Simon and Schuster, 1987.

———. *Giants and Dwarfs.* New York: Simon and Schuster, 1990.

Blumenthal, Sidney. *The Rise of the Counter-Establishment: From Conservative Ideology to Political Power.* New York: Times Books, 1986.

Bozell, Brent, III. *Weapons of Mass Distortion: The Coming Meltdown of the Liberal Media.* New York: Crown, 2004.

Britt, Lawrence. "Fascism Anyone?" *Free Inquiry* 23, no. 2 (2003). Web.

Brock, David. *Blinded by the Right: The Conscience of an Ex-Conservative.* New York: Crown, 2002.

———. *The Republican Noise Machine.* New York: Crown, 2004.

Brouwer, Steve. *Sharing the Pie: A Citizen's Guide to Wealth and Power in America.* New York: Henry Holt, 1998.

Callahan, David. *Fortunes of Change: The Rise of the Liberal Rich and the Remaking of America.* Hoboken: John Wiley and Sons, 2010.

Chait, Jonathan. "A Very Special Kind of Math." *Los Angeles Times,* April 19, 2005. Web.

———. *The Big Con: The True Story of How Washington Got Hoodwinked and Hijacked by Crackpot Economics.* Boston: Houghton Mifflin, 2007.

Chomsky, Noam, and Edward Herman. *Manufacturing Consent: The Political Economy of the Mass Media.* New York: Pantheon, 1988.

"Confessions of a Tobacco Lobbyist." *60 Minutes,* March 19, 1995. Burrell's transcripts.

Coulter, Ann. *Slander: Liberal Lies about the American Right.* New York: Three Rivers Press, 2002.

Douglass, Frederick. "Speech at Canandaigua, New York, Aug. 3, 1857." *"No Struggle, No Progress": Frederick Douglass and His Proverbial Rhetoric.* Edited by Wolfgang Mieder. New York: Peter Lang, 2001.

Frank, Thomas. *The Wrecking Crew: How Conservatives Rule.* New York: Metropolitan Books, 2008.

Franken, Al. *Lies and the Lying Liars Who Tell Them: A Fair and Balanced Look at the Right.* New York: Dutton, 2003.

Friedman, Thomas. *The World Is Flat: A Brief History of the Twenty-First Century.* New York: Farrar, Straus, and Giroux, 2005.

Goldberg, Bernard. *Bias: A CBS Insider Exposes How the Media Distort the News.* Washington, DC: Regnery, 2002.

Goldberg, Jonah. *Liberal Fascism: The Secret History of the American Left from Mussolini to the Politics of Meaning.* New York: Doubleday, 2007.

———. "The Rich Aren't Made of Money." *Los Angeles Times,* November 13, 2007. Web.

Hedrin, Sam. *Network.* New York: Pocket Books, 1976. Based on the screenplay by Paddy Chayefsky.

Horowitz, David. "The Intellectual Class War." In *The Art of Political War, and Other Radical Pursuits,* 115–122. Dallas: Spence, 2000.

Huxley, Aldous. *Brave New World and Brave New World Revisited.* New York: Harper, 1965.

Jefferson, Thomas. "The Natural Aristocracy." In *Writings.* Edited by Merrill D. Peterson. New York: Library of America, 1984.

Johnston, David Cay. *Perfectly Legal: The Covert Campaign to Rig Our Tax System to Benefit the Super Rich—and Cheat Everyone Else.* New York: Penguin, 2003.

Kozol, Jonathan. *Savage Inequalities: Children in America's Schools.* New York: Crown, 1991.

———. *Shame of the Nation.* New York: Crown, 2005.

Krugman, Paul. "For Richer." *New York Times Magazine,* October 20, 2002. Web.

———. *The Great Unraveling.* New York: W. W. Norton, 2004.

Laffer, Arthur B. "The Onslaught from the Left, Part I: Fact vs. Fiction." Laffer Associates, October 31, 2007. Web.

Lazere, Donald, ed. *American Media and Mass Culture: Left Perspectives.* Berkeley: University of California Press, 1987.

Lichter, S. Robert, Linda S. Lichter, and Stanley Rothman. *Watching America: What Television Tells Us about Our Lives.* Englewood Cliffs, NJ: Prentice Hall, 1991.

Lind, Michael. *Up from Conservatism.* New York: Free Press, 1996.

Macdonald, Dwight. *Against the American Grain.* New York: Random House, 1962.

Matalin, Mary, and James Carville, with Peter Knobler. *All's Fair: Love, War, and Running for President.* New York: Random House, 1994.

McChesney, Robert, and John Nichols. *The Death and Life of American Journalism: The Media Revolution That Will Begin the World Again.* New York: Nation Books, 2010.

"Movin' On Up: A Treasury Study Refutes Populist Hokum about 'Income Inequality.'" *Wall Street Journal,* November 13, 2007. Web.

Orwell, George. *Orwell's Nineteen Eighty-Four: Text, Sources, Criticism.* 2nd ed. Edited by Irving Howe. New York: Harcourt Brace Jovanovich, 1983.

———. "Politics and the English Language." In *Orwell's Nineteen Eighty-Four: Text, Sources, Criticism,* 2nd ed., edited by Irving Howe, 248–258. New York: Harcourt Brace Jovanovich, 1983.

Pollan, Michael. *The Omnivore's Dilemma.* New York: Penguin, 2006.

Rampton, Sheldon, and John Stauber. *Weapons of Mass Deception: The Uses of Propaganda in Bush's War on Iraq.* New York: Tarcher/Penguin, 2003.

Rank, Hugh. *Persuasion Analysis: A Companion to Composition.* Park Forest, IL: Counter-Propaganda Press, 1988.

Robinson, Eugene. "Tattered Dream: Who'll Tackle the Issue of Upward Mobility?" *Washington Post,* November 23, 2007. Web.

Safire, William. *Before the Fall.* New York: Doubleday, 1975.

Savio, Mario. "An End to History." In *Freedom's Orator: Mario Savio and the Radical Legacy of the 1960s,* edited by Robert Cohen, 329–332. New York: Oxford University Press, 2009.

Schlosser, Eric. *Fast Food Nation.* New York: Perennial, 2002.

Schor, Juliet. *The Overspent American: Why We Want What We Don't Need.* New York: Basic Books, 1998.

Sirotta, David. "The Neoliberal Bait and Switch." *In These Times,* September 11, 2010. Web.

Sklar, Holly. "Billionaires Up, America Down." McClatchy-Tribune News Service, October 17, 2007. Web.

Sommers, Christina Hoff. *Who Stole Feminism? How Women Have Betrayed Women.* New York: Touchstone, 1994.

Soros, George. "My Philanthropy." *New York Review of Books,* June 23, 2011: 12–16.

Stefancic, Jean, and Richard Delgado. *No Mercy: How Conservative Think Tanks and Foundations Changed America's Social Agenda.* Philadelphia: Temple University Press, 1996.

U.S. Treasury Department. *Income Mobility in the U.S. from 1996 to 2005.* Washington, DC: Government Printing Office, 2007. Web.

Weicher, John C. "Wealth-Gap Claptrap." *Weekly Standard,* July 1, 1996: 14–15.

Will, George. "What's Behind Income Disparity?" *San Francisco Chronicle,* April 25, 1995: A1.

Young America's Foundation. "America's Largest Campus Outreach Program." Web.

Index

AARP (American Association of Retired Persons), 89, 91, 92
ABC-Capital Cities-Paramount, 63
ad hominem, 20, 88, 94, 142, 145, 146, 147
ad populum, 142, 144
advertising, 93, 103–105
   children's, 108–109
   conflict of interest and, 87
   corporate, 103–105, 108–112
   food, 108–109
   news media and, 62–63
   political and advocacy, 106–108
   as propaganda, 103–105, 109–111
   social influence of, 109–111
Afghanistan, 4
Ailes, Roger, 73
Al Qaeda, 4
Alterman, Eric, 63
American Enterprise, 53
American Enterprise Institute, 55, 80
American-Israeli Public Affairs Committee (AIPAC), 97–98
American political spectrum, 33–35, 50, 71–73
Americans for Prosperity, 107

American Spectator, 53, 55, 82
analogies, 18
appeal to authority, 143
appeal to fear, 45, 77, 98, 120, 143
appeal to pity, 124, 135, 143, 149
appeal to the past or tradition, 143
Archer-Daniels-Midland, 109–110
argument from the converse, 26, 143–144
argument from the exception, 144
arguments
   circular, 144, 148
   downplaying, 19, 150
   economic, 115–140
   evaluation of, 16
   fallacious, 7–8
   guides for analyzing, 17–18
   playing up, 19, 150
   statistical, 124–129
Arthur Andersen, 7
Atlantic Monthly, 53
Atwater, Lee, 96

Bagdikian, Ben H., 52
bandwagon, 144
Barber, Benjamin, 98

Basic Books, 54
Beck, Glenn, 42, 69, 79, 95
begging the question, 144, 146
blaming the victim, 14, 146–147
Bleifuss, Joel, 93, 99
Bloom, Allan, 42–43, 55
Blue States, 48
Boorstin, Daniel, 105, 111, 143
Brave New Films, 83
Brock, David, 55, 56n1
Brouwer, Steve, 30, 92
Buchanan, Pat, 82
Buckley, William F., 53
Buffet, Warren, 42
Bush, George H. W., 26, 89, 96, 130–131
Bush, George W., 9, 27, 89, 99, 100, 115, 117, 126, 130–131

Callahan, David, 26
Canada, 30, 50
capitalism, 30–33, 36–39, 75, 92
Carroll, Jon, 56
Carville, James, 96
Cato Journal, 53
Center for American Progress, 55
Center for Science in the Public Interest (CSPI), 108
Chait, Jonathan, 117–119, 122
changing the subject, 144, 146, 149
Cheney, Richard, 89, 97
China, 33, 49
Chomsky, Noam, 71
Christmas, 113
circular argument, 144, 148
Citizens for a Sound Economy, 107
Citizens United case, 107
cleans and dirties, 2, 17–19, 24, 144–145
Clinton, Bill, 26, 27, 55, 117, 133
Clinton, Hillary, 26
Clooney, George, 33
CNN, 73, 75, 111
Coalition to Protect Seniors, 107
Cockburn, Alexander, 68–69
Colbert, Stephen, 73
Cold War, 44, 98, 137
Commentary, 53, 80
commentators, 34
common practice, 145, 150

communism, 28–30, 32, 37, 44–45, 50
compartmentalization, 17, 25, 44, 76–77, 95, 145, 149
conflict of interest, 85–90
confusion of cause and effect, 146
connotative language, 2–3, 19, 24, 68, 144
conservatism, 25–28, 33
conservatives, 30, 37–38, 47
    See also rightists and right wing
    connotation of, 3
    defense spending and, 98–99
    definition of, 24–25
    economic position of, 130–133
    in the media, 73
    social class and, 46–48
    tax policy of, 115–124, 126
Coulter, Ann, 2, 95
counterintelligentsia, 53, 54–55
Crawford, Victor, 96
C-SPAN, 78, 80
Cuba, 49
Current TV, 73

D'Amato, Al, 66
Davis, Gray, 68–69
definitions, ambiguity of, 67–71
demagoguery, 145
Democratic Leadership Council, 55
Democratic Party, 25–28, 33, 39, 41, 46–47, 71, 72
democratic socialists, 69
Department of Defense (DOD), 97–101
derision, 145
Disney, 63, 69, 77
distortion, 145
distraction, 142
Doonesbury, 33
double standard, 19, 98, 136, 145, 149, 150
doublethink, 145, 149
Douglass, Frederick, 11
downplaying, 19, 150
Dukakis, Michael, 96
Durst, Will, 82
Dyson, Michael Eric, 82

Eastern Europe, 49
economic arguments

analysis of, 115–140
  of conservatives, 130–133
  of liberals, 133–138
  statistical tricks and, 124–129
  on tax policy, 117–124
economic systems, 32–33, 36–37
Egypt, 49
Ehrenreich, Barbara, 82
Eisenhower, Dwight, 86, 97
either-or fallacy, 18, 27–28, 145
emotional appeals, 17–18, 146, 148, 149
Enron Corporation, 7
equal and opposite extreme, 63–64, 146
equivocation, 123, 146
ethnocentrism, 19, 73
evading the issue, 18, 146, 147, 148

Fahrenheit 9/11, 77
FAIR, 74
fallacious arguments, 7–8
false analogy, 55, 146
false dilemma, 145
false equation, 146
fascism, 31, 32, 37, 44–45, 50
faulty causation, 146–147, 148
Fillmore, Mallard, 33
flag-waving, 147, 149
flat tax, 118, 127, 131, 135–136
Forbes, Steve, 127
Fox, 69, 77
Fox News, 73, 79, 111
Frank, Thomas, 121
Franken, Al, 2
free enterprise, 32, 36, 38, 43
Free Press, 54
Free Speech Movement, 6–7
Friedman, Thomas, 72
FrontPage Magazine, 74

Gates, Bill, 41, 118, 126
General Electric, 98
Gibson, Mel, 33
Goldberg, Jonah, 117–120
Gore, Al, 27, 55, 73
government public relations, 96–101
government spending, 121, 130–131, 133, 135
government subsidies, 136–137

Green Party, 28, 71
Greenwald, Robert, 83
Guatemala, 49
guilt by association, 29, 96, 147
Gulf War, 98, 99

half-truths, 96, 147
Halliburton Industries, 97
Harper's, 53
Harris-Perry, Melissa, 82
hasty conclusions, 147, 148
Hayes, Chris, 82
Heritage Foundation, 55, 124
Herman, Edward, 71
Hightower, Jim, 68, 77, 82
Hill and Knowlton, 99
Hitler, Adolf, 45, 94–95, 103
Hollywood, 70, 76
Hoover, Herbert, 62
Hoover Institution, 55
Horowitz, David, 37
Huckabee, Mike, 73
Huffington, Arianna, 73
Huffington Post, 73
Hunt, H. L., 123
Hussein, Saddam, 8, 50, 99, 100
Huxley, Aldous, 94–95, 103, 109, 112
hype, 111–113

ideologues, 94
inadequate evidence, 147, 148
inconsistency, 142, 147
Indonesia, 49
inductive leap, 147, 148
Insight, 53
Intercollegiate Studies Institute, 55
invective, 95–96
Iraq, 4, 50
Iraq War, 4–5, 97, 99–100, 137
irrelevance, 147
Islamic terrorism, 50–51
Israel, 97–98
Israeli-Palestinian conflict, 51
Ivins, Molly, 82

Japan, 50
Jarvis, Howard, 9
Jefferson, Thomas, 62

jingoism, 147
Jobs, Steve, 41
Johnston, David Cay, 119
journals of opinion, 52–53, 80, 82

Kadlec, Daniel, 7–8
Kagan, Elena, 89
Kennedy, John, 133
Key, Wilson, 104
Keynesian economics, 133
Kinsley, Michael, 8–9
Koch, Charles, 42, 107
Koch, David, 42, 107
Kozol, Jonathan, 123, 124
Kristol, William, 53
Krugman, Paul, 121, 125
Kuwait, 50, 97, 99

labels, ambiguity of, 67–71
Labor Party, 71
Laffer, Arthur, 122
leftists and left wing, 41–44
   constituency of, 80
   differences from liberals and Democrats, 26, 28–42, 67–69, 71–77, 86–90, 130–138
   economic position of, 133–138
   patterns of rhetoric used by, 48–49
   positions of, 35–36
   radical, 69
   viewpoints of, in mass media, 80–83
Lehrer, Jim, 78
liberalism, 25–28, 33
liberals, 30, 38–39, 47
   See also leftists and left wing
   ambiguity of definition of, 67–68
   connotation of, 3
   defined, 24–25
   economic position of, 133–138
   in the media, 73
   social class and, 46–48
   tax policy of, 115–124, 126
Libertarian Party, 25
libertarians, 34, 35, 40, 44
Libya, 49
Lichter, Linda S., 69–70, 81
Lichter, S. Robert, 69–70, 81
Limbaugh, Rush, 69, 76, 79, 80, 82, 95, 96

lip service, 147, 150
loaded language, 2–3, 19, 24, 68, 144
lobbying, 91–93, 97–98
logical fallacies, 2, 18, 141–150
Los Angeles Times, 52, 72, 75
Lynch, Jessica, 100

Macdonald, Dwight, 60–61, 64
Maddow, Rachel, 82
Madison Center for Educational Affairs, 55
Maher, Bill, 73, 95
Marx, Karl, 29
Marxism, 28–29, 44
Matalin, Mary, 96
Matthews, Chris, 73, 76
McCain, John, 27, 115
media, 59–84
   advertising, 62–63, 87, 103–111
   bias in, 64, 66–83
   corporate ownership of, 63, 75, 77
   diverse influences in, 74–79
   employees, 75, 76, 87
   hype, 111–113
   news, 12–13, 33–35, 67–83, 111–112
   partisan, 2
   political spectrum and, 33–35
   political viewpoints in, 51–56
   public wants and, 60–65
   responsibility of, to inform, 62
   social media, 112
   target audience for, 61–62, 79
Media Education Foundation, 83
Media Matters, 74
Media Research Center, 74
Meyerson, Harold, 82
Middle East, 4, 49–50
Mieder, Wolfgang, 11
military-industrial-media complex, 96–101, 137
mixed economy, 40
Moore, Michael, 77, 82, 83, 95
Morris, Dick, 96
Moyers, Bill, 63, 77
MSNBC, 73, 82, 111
Murdoch, Rupert, 53, 63, 66, 73, 77, 82
Muslim world, 50–51

Myanmar (Burma), 49

NAACP (National Association for the Advancement of Colored People), 89
Nader, Ralph, 28, 82
name-calling, 18, 21, 95, 142, 146, 147–148
The Nation, 52–53
National Public Radio (NPR), 80
National Review, 53, 80
National Rifle Association (NRA), 90
Navasky, Victor, 52–53
Nazis, 32, 45, 94–95
NBC, 98
neoconservatives, 25
neoliberalism, 27, 50
New Left movement, 26
New Party, 71
New Republic, 52–53
News Corporation, 63
news media, 12–13, 75
   bias in, 66–83
   cable, 63, 111–112
   corporate ownership of, 63, 75, 77
   objectivity of, 66–67
   political spectrum and, 33–35
   profitability of, 62–63
   sensationalism and, 63, 112
New Yorker, 53
New York Post, 66
New York Times, 52, 72, 75
1984 (Orwell), 95, 112, 145
Nixon, Richard, 9
non sequiturs, 18, 142, 144, 147, 148
Norquist, Grover, 121
North American Free Trade Agreement (NAFTA), 27
North Korea, 49
Nye, Joseph, 98

Obama, Barack, 133
   election of, 13, 26
   labeling of, 3
   Supreme Court appointments by, 89
   tax policy of, 115, 117, 119, 126
O'Donnell, Lawrence, 73
Olbermann, Keith, 73, 95
Opensecrets.org, 91

optimism, 8–9
O'Reilly, Bill, 73
Orwell, George, 2, 11–12, 95, 97, 112, 145
overgeneralization, 13–14, 147, 148
oversimplification, 43, 142, 148

Packard, Vance, 104
Pakistan, 49
Palin, Sarah, 73
Palestinians, 51
Patients United Now, 107
Patriot missile, 98
PBS, 77, 80
Pearson, John, 122
Pentagon, 97–101
Peretz, Martin, 53
Perot, Ross, 28
personal attacks, 142, 145, 147
plain folks appeals, 124, 148
playing up, 19, 150
Plutocracy, 31, 32, 37, 38, 133
Podhoretz, John, 87
Podhoretz, Norman, 53
polemicists, ground rules for, 20–21
polemics, 95–96
Policy Review, 53, 80
political action committees (PACs), 92
political arguments
   evaluation of, 16
   guides for analyzing, 17–18
political attitudes, social class and, 46–48
political rhetoric, predictable patterns of, 48–49
political semantics, 24–25
political spectrum
   American, 33–35, 50
   relativity of viewpoint and, 71–74
   world, 30–33, 49–51
Pollan, Michael, 108
populism, 80
pork-barrel legislation, 89
post hoc reasoning, 18, 146
Poundstone, Paula, 82
Progressive Policy Institute, 55
propaganda, 7, 86, 91
   advertising as, 103–105, 109–111
   corporate, 93

propaganda *(continued)*
   defined, 148
   varieties of, 93–95
   wartime, 99–101
Proposition 13, 135
public broadcasting, 77–78
public relations, 91–93, 96–101

Qaddafi, Muammar, 98
quotation out of context, 148

radio
   commercial sponsorship of, 105
   public, 77–78
Random House, 54
Rank, Hugh, 18
rationalization, 17, 19
Reader's Digest, 79
Reagan, Ronald, 115, 117, 130–131, 133
Reagan Democrats, 26
Reaganomics. *See* supply-side economics
Reason, 53
red-baiting, 96
red herring, 146, 149
Red States, 48
reductionism, 18
reductive fallacy, 146
relativism, 71–74
Republican Party, 25–28, 33, 41, 47, 71, 72
resistance to change, 143
rhetoric
   defined, 2
   semantic calculator for bias in, 18–20
rhetorical fallacies, 141–150
rightists and right wing, 30, 31, 32, 35–36
Robertson, Pat, 82
Robinson, Eugene, 3
Rockefeller, Nelson, 26
Romney, Mitt, 78, 115
Rothman, Stanley, 69–70, 81
Rove, Karl, 73
Ryan, Joan, 108

Safire, William, 9
Saudi Arabia, 49, 50, 97

Savio, Mario, 6, 9, 22
Scaife, Richard Mellon, 55, 82
Scaife Foundation, 55
Scalia, Antonin, 89
scare tactics, 143
Schlosser, Eric, 108
Schor, Juliet, 64
Schumer, Charles, 66
selective vision, 19, 43, 69, 90, 95, 136, 145, 149, 150
self-contradiction, 147
self-fulfilling prophecy, 10, 105
semantic misunderstandings, 3
semantics, 2–3, 17, 24–25
sentimentality, 8, 19, 143, 149
September 11, 2001, 4, 9, 137
Sharpton, Al, 73
shifting ground, 144, 146, 149
Simon & Schuster, 54
Sirota, David, 76
Sklar, Holly, 122, 124, 127
slippery slope fallacy, 119, 146
smearing, 95–96
social class, political attitudes and, 46–48
social democracy, 30, 40, 69
socialism, 28–29, 31, 32, 36–37, 39–40
social media, 112
Social Security, 116, 119, 121
Sommers, Christina Hoff, 55
Sontag, Susan, 9
Soros, George, 42, 82
sources
   conflicts of interest in, 86–87
   political viewpoints in, 51–56
South Korea, 97
Soviet Union, 49, 137
special interests, 19, 85–90, 92, 107
special pleading, 7, 55, 85–90, 116–117, 149
stacking the deck, 19, 20, 24, 69, 86, 145, 147, 148, 150
statistical tricks, 124–129
Stauber, John, 93
Stewart, Jon, 73
straw man, 18, 145, 150
supply-side economics, 41, 115, 122, 124, 127, 131, 134

sweeping generalization, 148
Syria, 49

Taiwan, 97
talk radio, 12, 13
tax cuts, 115, 117, 126–127, 131, 134–136
tax policy, 116, 117–124, 126, 136
Tea Party, 27, 42, 107
television, 12–13, 64, 69–70
    cable, 63, 111–112
    commercial sponsorship of, 105
    public, 77–78
think tanks (research institutes), 54–56, 124
third parties, 28, 71
Thoreau, Henry David, 4
Tillman, Pat, 100
Time-Warner, 63, 75
tokenism, 150
Tomlinson, Kenneth, 77
too much or too little?, 146
transfer of authority, 143
tu quoque fallacy, 95, 146, 150
Turner, Ted, 75
TV Nation, 77
two-party system, 27–28
two wrongs make a right, 150

ultraconservatives, 32
unrepresentative sampling, 147, 148

vicious circle, 10–12

Vietnam, 49
Vietnam War, 99
viewpoints
    See also political viewpoints
    relativity of, 71–74
    spectrum of ideological, 30–33

Wag the Dog, 99
Wall Street Journal, 52, 63
Walton, Sam, 123
Washington Post, 52, 75
Washington Times, 52
watchdog organizations, 74
"we," 150
wealth gap, 117–124
Weekly Standard, 53, 80, 82
Weicher, John, 124–125
West, Allen, 96
Western Europe, 30, 50
Will, George, 119–120, 122, 123, 124
Wilson, Charles, 86
wishful thinking, 17, 19, 150
working class, 46–48
world political spectrum, 30–33, 49–51
World War II, 45

Young Americans for Freedom, 55
Young America's Foundation, 55

Zucchino, David, 100
Zuckerberg, Mark, 41